Signs in Life

Traveling together!

7-13-15

Signs in Life

Finding Direction in Our Travels with God

DEANNA NOWADNICK

Rhododendron
Books
Monroe, Washington

Signs in Life

Finding Direction in Our Travels with God

First printing 2015

ISBN 978-0-9835897-5-4
Library of Congress Control Number: 2015940768

Table of Contents

Acknowledgments ix

Prologue   This Way xv

Chapter 1   Yield 1

Chapter 2   School Zone 11

Chapter 3   Stop. 21

Chapter 4   Turn Right 31

Chapter 5   No U-Turn 41

Chapter 6   Milepost. 53

Chapter 7   Wrong Way 63

Chapter 8   Road Narrows 73

Chapter 9   One Way. 85

Chapter 10   Scenic Viewpoint 97

Chapter 11   Construction Zone 109

Epilogue   Divided Highway. 119

List of Photographs

Prologue   THIS WAY
            Kurt and Deanna's Wedding Get-Away • July 1981 xv

Chapter 1   YIELD
            Deanna's Freshman Year in College • September 1972. 1

Chapter 2   SCHOOL ZONE
            Deanna's Classroom at Emerson Elementary • March 1977. 11

Chapter 3   STOP
            Washington High School's *The Freedom Press* • February 1971. 21

Chapter 4   TURN RIGHT
            Kurt's Master's Degree Celebration • May 1983 31

Chapter 5   NO U-TURN
            Family's Christmas Picture • December 1989. 41

Chapter 6   MILEPOST
            Kurt and Deanna on Family Vacation • December 2003. 53

Chapter 7   WRONG WAY
            Family's Easter Picture • April 1990. 63

Chapter 8   ROAD NARROWS
            Deanna's Wedding Hankie • July 1981. 73

Chapter 9   ONE WAY
            Deanna's Book Appreciation Dinner • December 2011 85

Chapter 10 SCENIC VIEWPOINT
            Kurt and Deanna's Trip to New York City • October 2013 97

Chapter 11 UNDER CONSTRUCTION
            Kyle and Kevin's Afternoon in the Rain • March 1991. 109

Epilogue   DIVIDED HIGHWAY
            Kurt and Deanna's Trip to Cabo • February 2013 119

Dedication

In memory of Mom and Dad
who asked me to write a book never dreaming I'd write two

Acknowledgments

My Husband, Kurt

You mean the world to me. I am so grateful for your love and friendship. I continue to marvel at life's blessings. You may have been #65 on the football field, but you've always been #1 in my heart. As I said in the first book, your story has been intimately connected to my own story, and I thank you for allowing me to share it with the world.

My Children, Kyle and His Wife, Katie,
Kevin and His Wife, Manoela

When the four of us became the six of us, I was overjoyed. Kyle and Kevin, your father and I prayed that your lives might be filled with love and purpose. To see your days unfold with joy and wonder has given us both a renewed appreciation for God's love and faithfulness. Katie and Manoela, we treasure you both!

My Brother, David Thorp

How blessed I am to have you as my brother. Not until I wrote this book did I understand how you actually "got away" to college. I've watched you navigate life's construction zones without hitting the orange cones, dinging the paint, or denting the front end. You're a wise guy, and I mean that in the kindest, most complimentary way.

My Friends, Michol Phillips, Nancy Gustafson,
Cindy Brockhaus and Vicky Dugall

What started as a weekly cup of coffee has become so much more. I love our time together. You are thoughtful, honest, caring ladies! You've each enriched my life in a unique way. You are truly girlfriends inspired by God.

My Pastor, Robin Dugall
You teach. You encourage and push. You help me hear God in the words of a single Bible verse. You bring music out of my mangled, tangled attempt at a contemporary worship song with three sharps and a jazzy beat. I thank God that you were led to Peace Lutheran Church "for such a time as this."

My Peace Lutheran Church Critique Group
Orva Anderson, Pauline Barnekow, Merlaine Barnett, Sheryl Becker, Kirsten Carlson, Brad Feilberg, Cara Fleming, Lori Gese, Lynn Gose, Theresa Gose, Lawrence and Kimberlea Green, Nancy Gustafson, Linda Herman, Betty Hokana, Sue Kaikala, Ruth Koenig, Kurt and Kim Latimore, Donna Ludwig, Irene Lundquist, Amy Mann, Laila Nylund, Cathy Robbins, Chuck and Andi Swanson, Nancy Strain, and Laurie Yocum
I used to think of the term "church family" as religious-speak for folks in the pew Sunday morning. How wrong I was! I love that we get to do God's work together, that we get to share in a divinely-inspired journey. I will always appreciate your willingness to read through the book's rough manuscript together with me. Your comments were insightful, your suggestions excellent. Dan LeMay and Brandi Carter, dinners were grand!

My Publishing Team, Brenda Wilbee and Juanita Dix
Brenda, I wanted to grow as a writer, so I opened a Christian writer's guide and found your name at the top of the page. In my book, you are tops! Thank you for slogging through rewrites with me. Juanita, you're phenomenal! Your attention to detail and eye for design are unparalleled. The book is beautiful—inside and out. And honorable mention has to go to Darcy Johnson. You're not only a dear friend, but you're the best proofreader!

My Friend, Karen Kramer Farris
We've never met, yet your words of support have encouraged me. Your prayers have inspired me. I once told my son Kyle that cyber friends were not real friends. Not true. Not true at all!

My Boss, Jeffrey Ross
and Co-Worker, Ayana Meissner

Jeff, I thank you for including me in your practice these many years. Not only have I benefitted from all that you've sown professionally, but I've also gleaned wisdom and insight from those special corners in the field after the harvest. Ayana, doing what you do allows me to do what I do. You've enabled us to be the team we are. You're also a marvelous wife and mother with your own stories to tell!

My Traveling Companions

You're all a special part of my journey and the book. I will forever appreciate your place in my story. You are an amazing cast of characters and I'm grateful to you all.

Dr. Rodney Swenson, Professor, Pacific Lutheran University
Connie Scafturon, Parish Worker, Trinity Lutheran Church
Steve Kink, Political Organizer, Washington Education
    Association
Robert and Lorretta Elderkin, Founders, Pacific West
    Financial Group
Sheryl Wold, College Roommate and Lifelong Friend
Jeffrey Ross, President and Founder, The Planner's Edge
Tom Foster, Political Co-Conspirator and Religious
    Accomplice
Sue Collier, Owner, Self-Publishing Resources
Claudia Browers, College Dorm-Mate and Lifelong Friend
George and Phyllis Nowadnick, Beloved In-Laws
and Paesano's Coffee, Monroe's Best in the Land of Coffee

*"The LORD himself goes before you
and will be with you;
he will never leave you nor forsake you.
Do not be afraid;
do not be discouraged."*

Deuteronomy 31:8 (NIV)

This Way

One day, Moses was taking care of sheep and goats for his father-in-law Jethro, the priest of Midian, and Moses decided to lead them across the desert to Sinai, the holy mountain. There an angel of the LORD appeared to him from a burning bush. Moses saw that the bush was on fire, but it was not burning up. "This is strange!" he said to himself. "I'll go over and see why the bush isn't burning up."

When the LORD saw Moses coming near the bush, he called him by name, and Moses answered, "Here I am."

—Exodus 3:1-4 (CEV)

Prologue

"If you're going to ticket me, then ticket me!"

I scrambled out of the car, slammed the door, and kicked the rear tire. Squinting into the harsh glare of a flashlight, my first words were louder than necessary, "If you're going to ticket me, then ticket me! I just want to get home." Not giving the police officer a chance to respond, I continued, still annoyed, still defiantly frustrated, "I'm tired. Really—I just want to get home!"

"And I just need you to slow down, ma'am. I actually stopped you, because I really just needed you to slow down and stop—at the sign back there. You're in a school zone. It's dark. There's traffic."

The officer was right. Traveling home from the gym, I'd failed to stop at a busy corner. Distracted by a young mother's ever present to-do list, I'd rolled through an intersection, the middle school on my left, a railroad crossing on my right. Fortunately a man with a badge had cared enough to give me a much deserved warning and an undeniable lesson: road signs are an important part of safe travel.

Road signs are everywhere: SPEED LIMIT 25, SCHOOL ZONE, STOP. Yet even with signs telling us what to do and how best to do it, we still miss the signs, overlook and ignore them. But signs in life surround us for a reason and I've gotten costly reminders of their importance. A patrol car's red and blue flashing lights have refocused my attention on the speed limit—more than once. Traffic cameras have reminded me to slow down in a school zone—twice. And a police officer has re-emphasized the importance of coming to a complete stop at a busy intersection.

In addition to traffic signs, I have also overlooked and ignored directional signs. I live in Monroe, Washington, about an hour's drive from Seattle. On a trip into the city, I programmed my car's navigation system to get me from the freeway to a waterfront restaurant. After three turns, I decided I knew better than my digital guide. I didn't. I made wrong turn after wrong turn and silently cursed the afternoon's traffic. The delay cost me time and patience and taught me a second undeniable lesson: road signs are not just an important part of safe travel, but there are consequences when ignored and overlooked.

So why don't I follow the signs, block after block, turn after turn? Why don't I heed the high resolution images on my car's high definition screen? The signs were all there: a black and white sign alerting me to the speed limit, a red sign reminding me to stop, a yellow sign warning of the school zone. There were signs telling me of the exit ahead and the turn on my right. Still I ignored some, skipped others, and overlooked many. Why did I, *why do I*, ignore the help?

And if I struggle to get around the block, how will I ever survive the bigger journey? How will I navigate life? Not the quick trip to the grocery store, but the longer journey through adulthood? Not only the daily commute, but the more onerous trek through times of trial? Not just the trip into the city, but the turn into temptation? What about my travels as a wife and mother, sister and friend? What about my travels with God?

I really do want to follow God more closely, but I've repeatedly ignored the spiritual guidance that could've helped me in my quest. Too many times I thought I knew more, knew better. At other times I overlooked God's directional signs and tuned out the audible instructions coming from life's metaphorical console. And then there were those times I just didn't pay attention.

I'm not alone. People long ago and people today, we've all sought to follow God more closely. The Bible shares example after example, stories that also remind us of our propensity to miss the signs. We question where we're going. We complain about our circumstances. In a story that spanned four decades, God led His chosen people, the Israelites, through the wilderness with a pillar of smoke by day and a pillar of fire by night, huge THIS WAY signs. Their leader, Moses, even encountered personal signs when he saw a burning bush and heard the voice of God. All these signs were important as God directed and redirected Moses and more than 600,000 Israelites on a journey that would take them from Egyptian slavery to the Promised Land.

God's been active in all our lives, directing and redirecting. Through Bible stories and our own personal experiences, we see the signs. Through Bible stories and our own travels through life, we learn that God doesn't just issue a citation and move on to the next offender. He steers us toward Him and His divine purpose, toward that promised place He has for each one of us. The man with the badge cared enough to warn me and cite me. God cares enough to guide me and direct me. And when I mess up? When we mess up? He forgives and redeems, redirects and refocuses—just as He did with Moses and the Israelites. And that's a good thing, because I don't know about you, but I need help and guidance. Often.

So here's what you also need to know. I battle weight issues. My walk is a nagging reminder of past knee and hip surgeries. I place way too much importance on mascara and hair gel. My driving record lists way too many infractions. I get dazed and confused in places unfamiliar to me, also in places I know well. I can obsess over the smallest details, especially the insignificant and inconsequential. I make mistakes. I wander off. I overlook the signs and miss the turn.

Moses and the Israelites made mistakes, too. On their journey to the Promised Land, they overlooked signs and missed turns. Their story is similar to my own in many ways, but strikingly different in others. I've never known the brutality of slavery, never been forced from my home. I've never had to walk through a desert, never been nomadic. I've never been a camper for goodness sakes! Still God's traveled with all of us wherever we've been and wherever we've been going.

> "Our travels with God are part of His story,
> His purpose, travels that begin right now."
> —Robin Dugall

Signs in Life tells of my journey and the divine signs I've encountered along the way. In my travels, there have been directional signs, mileposts, and cautionary signs. There have been exit signs and speed limit signs. There have been signs that were seen and others that were heard. All have helped me follow God and find His purpose for my life. By sharing the signs in my life, I hope you'll be able to see the signs in yours. I might be speeding through a stop sign—again!—while you're navigating a busy street, but our journeys are very similar. I think we all want to be part of a greater purpose. We all want help and guidance in our understanding of God and His plans for us. And when we miss the signs, real and divine, we want to know that God will redirect and refocus us, that He will get us back on track. My pastor, Robin Dugall says, "Life with God is not just about a heavenly destination. Our travels with God are part of His story, His purpose, travels that begin right now."

Whenever we got in the car, I used to tell my boys, "Buckle up. We're going for a ride." In life we're all going for a ride. Our travels with God are an adventure in discovery and growth, an opportunity for each one of us to repeat the words of Moses, "Here I am."

THIS WAY. This is my story, the signs in my life. So far.

Deanna Nowadnick

Yield

"I am sending you to lead my people out of this country."

But Moses said, "Who am I to go to the king and lead your people out of Egypt?"

God replied, "I will be with you. And you will know that I am the one who sent you, when you worship me on this mountain after you have led my people out of Egypt."

—Exodus 3:10-12 (CEV)

Chapter 1

"I—don't—want—to—go—to—PLU!"

I looked left in alarm at blinking turn signals. A tractor-trailer was moving into my lane on the interstate—not ahead of me, not behind me, right into me! The driver didn't see me. I honked, but he didn't hear me. I needed to get out of his way, but no sooner had I swerved onto the shoulder than I looked up in panic at a narrow overpass just ahead. No shoulder! I had to stop! I had to stop now! Slamming on the brakes, I came to a dramatic halt, my heart racing, body shaking, tears streaming down my cheeks.

I watched the truck disappear into the distance. The driver had never seen me. He'd never heard me honk. Yet despite his failure to yield, he'd unknowingly kept me safe. His yellow blinking lights had given me time to get out of danger.

The incident had been so unexpected. I'd been traveling along at my own pace in my own lane to my own destination, never expecting a close encounter with danger. That day I learned the frightening consequence of someone's careless failure to yield. In my personal life, I'd learn the same.

I have to admit, with less drama but more frequency, I've been the careless driver. I've been the one to disobey the rules of the road. Not long ago I was coming home from the office and I found myself thinking about everything but my driver's blind spot. When I moved to change lanes, the blare of a horn startled me. I was close enough to catch the eye of an alarmed driver. I grimaced and mouthed the words, "*Oops, sorry!*" Not long after the incident I had to apologize again. This time the blare of a horn went unheeded, and I proceeded to back out of a parking space right into a late model SUV, a metal-on-metal jolt that got my immediate attention. I could only sigh, get out of the car, and extend my hand in a conciliatory gesture. The unhappy driver was not interested in a handshake. He just wanted my contact information and the phone number for my insurance company. I don't blame him. Moments when we fail to yield, when we're at fault, are difficult. They give us an unexpected jolt, but then that's to be expected when we fail to yield.

And when we don't, there are consequences. On the freeway I had to get out of the way of a truck or risk serious injury. In the parking garage I had to deal with an unhappy driver and his crunched fender, an accident that cost me a little self-respect and a few "good driving" points. When my own petulant determination forced me off the road as a teenager, my failure to yield had its own consequences. My parents saw it all firsthand.

Unlike the truck driver who never noticed me, my parents were very aware of the lane in which I'd been traveling and they were not pleased. After suffering through my turbulent teen years, Mom and Dad were determined to rein in my "*Don't tell me what to do!*" attitude with Pacific Lutheran University's promise of "a quality education in a Christian context." My response had been a rebellious "I—don't—want—to—go—to—PLU!"

Rebellious? Petulant? Recalling those miserable discussions, I think it's more accurate to say petulant. By the time I'd finished high school, Mom and Dad were reeling. If they'd asked me to be home at midnight, I'd walk in the door at 12:15. If they'd asked me to drive straight home after the football game, I'd add three stops—using Dad's truck and Dad's gas. If they'd asked about my day, I'd roll my eyes and snip, "It was fine." I wanted all the privileges of young adulthood and none of the responsibilities. I wanted to do what I wanted to do when I wanted to do it. My parents were desperate to get past the antics and the drama, and

I was frantic to get past PLU as an option. After growing up just two short blocks from the university, I wanted to get away—to *any* school but PLU. As a child, I'd been chased out of the school's flowering plum trees when I'd been caught climbing with friends. During the school's NO BIKES era, I'd been escorted off campus after getting caught racing my ten-speed between dorms. By the time I graduated from high school, my battle-fatigued parents were hoping the people who'd kept their daughter out of the trees and off her bike would be able to give her the restraint and guidance they felt she desperately needed. And that's what I feared most: restraint and guidance.

My parents needed no blinking lights or honking horn to signal where they were going, or more precisely, where I was going. They had only to quietly remind me that they were footing the bill for this college adventure, and my objections were quickly dismissed. Mom and Dad knew where they wanted me to be. They knew the lane in which I'd been traveling as a teen and wanted to steer me clear of any higher education fender benders or more serious accidents. I needed to yield as I merged into college life, and I was *not* happy about it.

Actually, I was angry. I was angry that Mom and Dad had refused to consider any school but PLU. I was angry that I wasn't getting my way and getting away. I was angry that God had obviously sided with my parents in the decision-making process. Clearly those prayers had been for naught. I felt divinely let down and terribly frustrated. When the time came to move into my new dorm room, I fussed and fumed all the way down the street and around the corner. But by the time I'd thrown the last of my clothes into a dresser drawer, I'd already begun mapping out a plan. Mom and Dad may have chosen where I'd attend school, but I'd choose how to proceed. Determined not to give in, determined to hold my place in the fast lane, determined not to yield to anyone about anything, I skipped classes, shrugged off homework assignments, and jumped into the social scene.

Missing from my hastily thrown together plan was any accountability. My German 101 professor would change that. Dr. Rodney

Swenson began class at 7:50 a.m. Monday through Friday. Had it not been for the early hour, I would've found him entertaining and engaging. With a twinkle in his eye and a lopsided smile, Dr. Swenson bounced into our classroom each day with a cheery *"Guten Morgen! Wie geht es Dir?"* My head heavy, my eyes barely open, I'd invariably jerk upright in response. How was I?

How was I? Truthfully, most days I was exhausted, rarely getting enough sleep the night before, nor could I seem to get those pesky homework assignments done. Tired and unprepared, I was having trouble with attendance before the end of our first month together. When Dr. Swenson phoned after an extended streak of absences, I listened in stunned silence.

"Fraulein, you've missed a lot of class. Have you been ill? I worry that you're getting behind. We're proceeding through the material quickly. We're learning new vocabulary words every day." Dr. Swenson went on to detail my scholarly shortcomings. When he finally paused for a reply, I could only mumble something incoherent *auf Deutsch.*

Later at lunch with friends, I embarked on a ridiculous diatribe. "Guess who called and woke me up this morning? *Herr Swenson!* My German professor actually called my room looking for me!" In a tone of exasperation, I rolled my eyes and went on, "He said I've missed a lot of class. Should I also remind him that I've missed a lot of homework? Anyway—he wants me back—in class—tomorrow."

What I didn't say in my rant? Lessons in the conjugation of verbs were about to be replaced by lessons in responsibility and accountability. So far my travels on the academic interstate had not gone well, and now Dr. Swenson had come alongside me, horn honking, lights blinking. I had to stop! Now! Remembering the plan I'd mapped out while moving into the dorm, I heaved a sigh of resignation. I hadn't thought to factor in a professor's own determination that I attend class and get my work done. Dr. Swenson had made it very clear that I'd need to pay attention to the road I was now traveling. I'd need to yield, get back into class, and finish those pesky homework assignments.

> While the Bible doesn't talk specifically about the
> challenges of college, it does have something to
> say about our struggles in defeat.

By the end of my freshman year, I'd see the signs more clearly: defiance was not going to mesh with the life of a college student intent on graduating in four years. The young woman who'd finished high school with honors was now trying to explain C- grades to her concerned parents. My rebellious plan had only hurt myself, and I was now in a figurative heap at the side of the road—disappointed, dispirited, my pride and self-worth bruised. The year had come to a dramatic conclusion of substandard work and misplaced determination with my heart racing, body shaking, tears streaming down my cheeks.

While the Bible doesn't talk specifically about the challenges of college, it does have something to say about our struggles in defeat. Jesus even tells about a traveler who'd been beaten, robbed, and left for dead at the side of the road. Others passed him by, but a Samaritan took pity, first tending his wounds and then taking him to an inn where he could heal. Before leaving, the Good Samaritan gave the innkeeper money for expenses, promising to return and settle up should there be additional costs.

When I found myself beaten down by disappointment and frustration, robbed of my pride and self-worth, feeling broken and dispirited, I got help from my own Good Samaritan. Connie, a caring church worker, got me a part-time office job at Trinity Lutheran Church, the church where I'd grown up, the church across the street from my dorm. Working with her on Saturdays and weekdays after class, I became the model of decorum and professionalism, leaving the rude, snippy, self-absorbed teenager behind for a few hours each week. While I typed and filed and answered the phone, I healed from the petulant, rebellious, defiant times of my youth. In a small church office, Connie gave me the fresh start I sorely needed. I got to assume a new role, put on a new identity. No longer was I the daughter coming home late, the student missing another day of class. I was the part-time assistant who prepared and printed the Sunday worship bulletin efficiently and capably. I was the young person who could finesse the temperamental Gestetner mimeograph machine and the antiquated Addressograph. I enjoyed wonderful feelings of accomplishment. While learning to drink very strong, very black coffee, I learned to answer the phone with poise and self-assurance. I also learned to expect more of myself.

Moses had to learn to expect more, too. Pressed into God's service as the Israelite's leader, he balked. And in his situation, who wouldn't? God was pushing him in a direction not anticipated, in a direction fraught with danger. Moses had been adopted and raised by Pharaoh's daughter after being found in bulrushes as a baby. His royal upbringing positioned him for national leadership in Pharaoh's "Great House," but life had taken a dramatic turn when he killed an Egyptian for beating an Israelite slave. Fleeing punishment and in exile, Moses encountered God in a burning bush. There God asked him to yield in a way he never could've imagined, to lead in a way he never could've foreseen. Moses was to deliver God's people from slavery!

Had I been in his sandals, I would have done more than just balk. I would have had a major meltdown in the middle of that hot and dusty desert, overheating in front of the burning bush, blowing a gasket over the extraordinary, inconceivable, mind-boggling instructions I'd just been given. In my little part-time job, I'd had my own worries and concerns. Given a new direction, I didn't want to fail. I didn't want to fall short of expectations. I didn't want to let Connie down. And I certainly didn't want to mess up in church. Listening to God speak from a flaming bush, I can only imagine how Moses must have felt. Startled? No doubt about it. Anxious? Most likely. Frightened? Perhaps. Overwhelmed? Definitely. Ready to go? Hmmm...

Are we ever ready to follow God? Let's face it, God can send us in directions we never imagined. He believes in us in ways we don't. We fall back on our perceived strengths aware of past weaknesses. Some days we complain at being told what to do; other days we cry out for guidance. So often I've done both. And then we remember God's promise to Moses, a promise for us all, "I will be with you."

At the corner of 121st Street and Park Avenue in Parkland, Washington, are two signs: Pacific Lutheran University on the one side and Trinity Lutheran Church on the other. I also imagine a YIELD sign, a cautionary sign that became important to my personal journey. When college decisions were being made, I thought I knew best. I thought I knew better than anyone where I needed to go to school. God used the determined efforts of my parents to get me where my unruly, petulant self needed to be. He used a professor's persistence to awaken me to my academic responsibilities. And when I lay defeated in a heap of self-pity, my pride wounded, God met me at the side of the road with a church worker. All helped me grow up personally and spiritually. As I merged into adulthood, God placed YIELD signs along the way. I'd tried desperately to "get away," to do it my way, but God had come alongside and shown me His way.

Rest Area

1. Have you ever found yourself just wanting to do what you wanted to do when you wanted to do it?

2. In what circumstances have you had to yield in your daily travels with God?

3. Have there been times when you've needed to expect more of yourself?

4. Have you had a personal Good Samaritan?

5. When God speaks, how do you get ready to go?

School Zone

Moses replied, "I have never been a good speaker. I wasn't one before you spoke to me, and I'm not one now. I am slow at speaking, and I can never think of what to say."

But the LORD answered, "Who makes people able to speak or makes them deaf or unable to speak? Who gives them sight or makes them blind? Don't you know that I am the one who does these things? Now go! When you speak, I will be with you and give you the words to say."

Moses begged, "LORD, please send someone else to do it."

The LORD became irritated with Moses and said, "What about your brother Aaron, the Levite? I know he is a good speaker. He is already on his way here to visit you, and he will be happy to see you again. Aaron will speak to the people for you, and you will be like me, telling Aaron what to say. I will be with both of you as you speak, and I will teach each of you what to do. Now take this walking stick and use it to perform miracles.

—Exodus 4:10-17 (CEV)

Chapter 2

"Wow! How did you ever catch that snake?"

The light flashed again. For the second time in two months, a traffic camera caught me speeding through a school zone—same spot, same camera, same speed. After paying $124 for the first infraction, you'd think I'd have learned my lesson. No. Once again I'd been caught driving too fast through the crosswalk of my neighborhood's elementary school. Two weeks later, when my second citation arrived, a photo of my license plate identified me as a speeding transgressor of the city's traffic regulations.

SCHOOL ZONE signs are extremely important. They identify areas where children are present, where the consequences of going too fast can be grave. They're especially important to those of us who speed—again and again. SCHOOL ZONE signs were also important to my personal life. They not only identified places where children were present, but places where I'd need to slow down professionally.

But somehow I'd missed the signs.

Looking back, the signs had been quite clear. In 1976 I was a struggling student teacher in an eighth-grade Language Arts classroom. My unit on poetry had fallen flat. Led Zeppelin lyrics had failed to engage my students. Their less-than-enthusiastic response to "Ooh, it makes me wonder/Ooh, it makes me wonder" forced me to wonder if "Stairway to Heaven" was really exemplary poetry. But rather than question my teaching skills, I'd simply concluded that Language Arts was not "my thing."

A second sign followed shortly. At the end of the term I moved into a Special Education classroom, but sitting with squirmy, squirrelly teenagers five and six years behind in reading and math, I was just as uncomfortable. I looked across my desk into anxious eyes that reflected frustration, disappointment, and confusion, eyes now questioning my own ability to help. My middle-school students still didn't know their vowel sounds. They still didn't know their multiplication tables. *What can I possibly do in a fifty-minute class period? In the next six weeks?* I was overwhelmed and didn't see that my difficulties with these struggling students reflected my own struggles with whether or not to teach. Instead I sped past another cautionary sign that should've slowed me down. I simply dismissed my doubts, this time chalking it up to inexperience.

By the time I finished student teaching and graduated from PLU with a Bachelor's in Education, I'd managed to overlook, ignore, and deny two cautionary SCHOOL ZONE signs. I'd successfully talked myself into believing that I just needed to get into my own classroom and all would be copacetic, as my mom, the teacher, used to say.

Three months later I was excited to accept my first teaching job. After graduation I'd been waitressing at the Butcher, Baker, Candlestick Maker, a local "medieval" restaurant. My customers were luncheon diners who wanted quick service and wonderful pleasantries along with cheap gruel and grog. Waitressing was harder than I'd imagined, and every day I'd had to renew my vow to be pleasant and appreciative. One day after splitting a check eight ways and finding an undeservedly small tip, I was feeling neither pleasant nor appreciative. I marched out of the dining room in search of my manager. It was time to let him know I was moving on.

"Don, I've been meaning to tell you, I'm going to be a teacher."

"A teacher? Wait! You told me you wanted to be a waitress!"

"No, I actually have a degree in education. I just got a teaching job in Snohomish. I start in three weeks, so I need to give notice."

After an unbearably long silence, he muttered, "That's great. You're definitely no waitress."

I hadn't expected a parting gift, but after months serving up soup and salad dressed as a wench, I was at least hoping for a rousing "Go get 'em, Teach!"

That I needed encouragement was telling. I was naïve, thinking I only needed an extra helping of hope and excitement to inspire me, but I'd missed the signs as a student teacher. Now I'd missed this third sign as I left the restaurant and sped into my new classroom. School was starting in less than a month. I had bulletins boards to plan and desks to arrange. I stepped on the accelerator, not realizing that I was rushing toward uncertainty, discontent, and unhappiness.

> But God has given us the ability to think and feel,
> heartfelt and mindful reactions that can spur us on
> or give us pause.

It's easy to overlook, ignore, and deny cautionary signs in our professional lives. We're expected to know where we're going and how we're going to get there. Some questions make for polite conversation; some are more pointed: *Where are you going to school? When are you going to graduate? Where are you going to live? You're doing what?* The questions continue: *When are you starting your family? How long will you stay? When are you going to retire? You're doing what?* Not wanting to answer, "I don't know," not wanting to appear lost or unsure, I hurried past signs that should've slowed me down. I'd gotten started on the teaching track and just didn't know how and where to make a change.

But God has given us the ability to think and feel, heartfelt and mindful reactions that can spur us on or give us pause. At times we feel exhilarated and confident, other times cautious and uneasy. At times we "hear" a quiet voice of reason; at other times we "see" more clearly. And then there are those times when we just disconnect, ignoring the tug on our hearts, not bothering to "get our head around" the situation.

Three weeks later I stood outside my classroom door greeting students the first day of school.

"Hi, I'm Miss Thorp. Can I help you find your classroom?"

"Hi, I'm Miss Thorp. I'll be teaching reading and math."

"Hi, I'm Miss Thorp. I'm new, too."

Yes, Miss Thorp, the new teacher, the school's first Learning Disabilities instructor. I'd been hired to work with students in second through sixth grade, kids who were starting to fall behind in reading and math. Remembering my hopelessness with middle school underachievers, I was excited to know that I'd now get to be first on the scene with remedial instruction. As the days rolled by, I focused on the positives of teaching. I adored my kids. I enjoyed the staff camaraderie. I took pride in my bulletins boards and reading group preparations. I ignored the nagging feeling that something was amiss, that I might not belong in teaching. I wasn't ready to admit that I enjoyed preparing my lessons more than teaching them, liked staff meetings more than morning recess, preferred organizing adults more than children, excelled at putting together agendas more than math quizzes. I avoided the truth for four years, and then came an unavoidable sign. A cold-blooded reptile, a scaly, legless vertebrate, an air-breathing creepy, crawly thing finally got my attention.

"Miss Thorp! Miss Thorp! Norman has a snake! Miss Thorp, Norman found a snake at recess!"

I looked up from my desk to see a proud fourth-grader strutting into our classroom holding a garter snake by the tail. While Norman smiled in sheer delight and the snake bobbed in sheer frustration, I knew I had mere nanoseconds to calmly and professionally respond to my student's playground discovery or forever be plagued by writhing reptiles of all shapes and sizes.

I tried to smile. "Wow, Norman! How did you ever catch that snake? You must have been very alert and very fast!" Starting to feel panic ooze through my persona of calm, I continued quickly, "Norman, I think we need to find a place back on the playground where your snake can do whatever snakes enjoy doing."

"But, but..."

"Don'tcha think your snake will be happier outside? Look at him. He's rather frantic, don'tcha think?" The snake was indeed squirming from its upside down position, frantically thrashing in a valiant, yet futile attempt to right itself and find ground. The reptile was small, but bobbing in discomfort—and no doubt, fear—it seemed huge, a sad scene where unhappy snake meets overly excited ten-year old and panicked teacher.

Too busy trying to hang on, Norman could only nod in agreement as the snake continued throwing itself in every direction. Realizing Norman's grip had to have been tenuous at best, I suggested going to the playground—now. Together we walked back down the hall, both of us silent. I'm not sure what Norman was thinking. I was just praying that God would keep the thing in Norman's grip. Recalling the incident later in the day, I said aloud for the first time, "Dear God, what am I doing in a classroom?"

A difficult moment. I'd missed the signs as a student teacher, and then I'd ignored my need for undue validation speeding into my first classroom. Now I'd just admitted out loud that I'd made a big mistake. Remembering Alexander's wail of frustration in a favorite children's book, it was a terrible, horrible, no good, very bad day. And like Alexander who'd had gum in his hair, I'd had a snake in my classroom and was ready to move to Australia. Looming large was my parents' reaction. They'd paid a high price for my "quality education in a Christian context." Mom would worry and Dad would want to have a talk, because looming larger was the real question: if not a teacher, what?

Doubt shook me to my core. I thought an education degree would bring me a Nordstrom-sized paycheck, medical, dental, and orthodontia coverage, and a nice retirement of European travel after those thirty copacetic years in the classroom. Personal satisfaction had never been considered. Now a writhing reptile had me shivering in doubt and uncertainty. I didn't know what to do. I didn't know which way to turn.

So I cried. My earlier feelings of revulsion mirrored unconscious fear and apprehension. My tears were a heartfelt, conscious reaction to what felt like an enormous situation. My earlier walk down the hall may have been about getting a snake outside, but it had really been the first steps in a much bigger journey, a journey that felt epic in size. My reptilian SCHOOL ZONE sign hadn't just slowed me down; it had stopped me in my tracks. Frightened and discouraged, uncertain and frustrated, I finally found my professional brakes, but not before colliding with unavoidable concerns. I had rent to pay. I had a car loan. My Nordstrom bill was due on the 15th.

And then my parents asked the question we'd all been avoiding, "So what are you going to do?"

Calming words came from the man who'd one day become my husband. "It's going to be okay. It's going to work out." Kurt's words were a vague reference to my future, but his reassurance was a specific belief in me. Shuddering through the end of yet another cry, I had no idea what I'd do after June, but that day I didn't need to know. I was ready to give my notice and trust that my professional future would be okay. More importantly, I was ready to trust in something, someone, bigger than myself. I was ready to acknowledge that God might have a better plan for me.

Trust. Moses had to learn to trust, too. When God asked him to lead the Israelites out from under Egyptian tyranny, Moses didn't know where he'd be going or how he'd be geting there. Despite growing up the adopted child of Egyptian royalty, he'd had to flee his homeland a murderer. Now God was pulling him into a huge leadership position, one he hadn't asked for, hadn't expected, didn't want. Moses knew Pharaoh's power first hand. God wasn't just suggesting Moses change careers; He was changing the course of Moses' life and the lives of the Israelites. Yet despite God's assurances, Moses was reluctant. Leading the Israelites to freedom would require not only his trust in God, but the people's trust in him.

"So, God, what if the people don't believe me? What if they say, 'The LORD didn't appear to you'?"

"What's that in your hand? Throw it to the ground."

Moses threw down his staff and immediately jumped back. "A snake!"

"Reach out and grab it by the tail."

Moses grabbed the snake and it turned back into his staff.

"They'll believe," said the LORD.

Quite a chat. I've wondered about Moses' reaction. At any point did he have a "snake in the classroom" moment? At any time did he shake his head and think, *What am I doing here? What am I doing in front of a burning bush?* Did he turn to his brother Aaron and say, "I'm having a terrible, horrible, no good, very bad day. I think I'm going to Australia. Would you talk to God?"

Both Moses and I faltered when life changed direction. Moses didn't know where he'd be going and neither did I. Prompted by unavoidable signs, we put our foot on the brakes. With writhing reptiles, God had gotten our attention and then He'd shared lessons in trust: "I will be with you... I will teach you..."

For Moses, trust was critical. Shortly after he and the Israelites fled Egypt, Pharaoh sent his army marching after them! The Red Sea was before them! Cornered, the people cried out in fear. Their faith would be put to the test. They'd all need to trust in God's plans for them.

For me, trust would also be critical as I walked out of my classroom. With Norman and his classmates, we'd worked on vowel sounds and multiplication tables. We'd had days that were thought-provoking and eye-opening and some that were not. When I left in June, I knew I'd done my best, but I needed to move on. Watching the buses pull away on the last day of school, I found myself at the shores of my own Red Sea, uncertain prospects in front of me and unshakeable doubts in hot pursuit. My faith was going to be tested. I was going to need God to part some waters, but first I was going to need to stop, stand firmly in the sand, and trust in His guidance.

Rest Area

1. Where have you needed to slow down in your travels with God?
2. Any places in life where you've needed to slow down more than once?
3. How have you been able to get through a "terrible, horrible, no good, very bad day"?
4. Has God ever had to use a "snake" to get your attention?
5. Have you ever found yourself at the shore of your own Red Sea?

Stop

R. TED BOTTIGER, Pierce, part

When the Israelites saw the king coming with his army, they were frightened and begged the LORD for help. They also complained to Moses, "Wasn't there enough room in Egypt to bury us? Is that why you brought us out here to die in the desert? Why did you bring us out of Egypt anyway? While we were there, didn't we tell you to leave us alone? We had rather be slaves in Egypt than die in the desert!"

But Moses answered, "Don't be afraid! Be brave, and you will see the LORD save you today. These Egyptians will never bother you again. The LORD will fight for you, and you won't have to do a thing."

The LORD said to Moses, "Why do you keep calling out to me for help? Tell the Israelites to move forward. Then hold your walking stick over the sea. The water will open up and make a road where they can walk through on dry ground."

—Exodus 14:10-16 (CEV)

Chapter 3

"Dear God, what am I doing here?"

My father and I climbed into his 1969 Chevrolet C-10 Fleetside long-bed pickup with me behind the wheel. Teaching me to drive was a magnanimous gesture: he'd kept his beloved truck impeccably maintained, the chrome and aluminum grille spotless, the cab clean and like new. I was fifteen and knew there was nothing about me that was impeccably maintained as far as Dad was concerned. We'd argued over mascara and blue eye shadow and jeans that were too tight. We'd clashed over my snippiness and attitude of entitlement. My father had to have been dreading the prospect of me driving.

For our first lesson Dad took me to a very long, very straight stretch of highway just outside town. After I'd taken the truck's Powerglide automatic transmission from park to drive, Dad began his instructions.

"Okay, now. Check your mirrors. Give it a little gas—"

I plopped my foot on the accelerator and slammed backward into the bench seat as the truck jerked ahead.

Dad's response was immediate, "You're going a little fast."

A minute later, his directions were more emphatic. "Slow down. The sign may say 45, but you don't need to be going that fast."

Nearing an intersection, Dad pointed and said, "Why don't you turn right at the next corner?"

I can only assume Dad expected me to slow down and stop before making the turn. Speeding toward the bright red, impossible-to-miss STOP sign, Dad shouted, "You need to brake!" but it was too late. I was going too fast and couldn't make a complete turn. I careened through the intersection, the truck landing in gravel on the opposite side of the road.

Waiting for the dust to settle, Dad sighed, the sound of his exasperation filling the pickup's small cab. I'd been driving mere minutes, flying down the road, not heeding a single direction. And now, I'd just sped past my first STOP sign. Sighing again, Dad grumbled, "Keep it in park. I'm going to need a couple minutes."

Dad got out and began a slow walk around the truck, his displeasure evident with every step. I winced, knowing Dad had really just needed a few minutes to see what the gravel had done to his truck's yellow-green paint and Blue Coral® hand-waxed shine.

Years later and all grown up, my foot was still on the gas when I sped down the road from one job to another, this time missing several professional STOP signs. Facing the Red Sea, Moses had stopped and trusted in God for direction. Facing my own Red Sea of career choices, I plunged in. If I could organize a classroom, I was certain I could organize the next phase of my life—without help from friends, counsel from Mom and Dad, or direction from God. I wasn't even sure how to include God in my plans. Add a prayer or two or three to the day? Meet with Christian girlfriends for coffee? Make sure to be in church on Sunday? It was just easier to keep going and not think about God.

I watched the buses depart on the last day of school, knowing I'd soon follow. The bulletin boards had been taken down, the textbooks stored. I'd boxed up my fear and anxiety, excited for the new challenge of a job in politics. Getting behind the wheel of my 1978 light blue Chevrolet Monte Carlo, I stepped on the gas, making only the briefest hesitation at the parking lot's STOP sign. I was on my way to Olympia, Washington's state capital, where I'd be serving as a campaign coordinator for the Washington Education Association (WEA), the state's largest teachers' union. I'd be organizing teachers in the support of local candidates running for state and national office. Together we'd be doorbelling neighborhood precincts and calling voters to get out and vote. I was thrilled! *This* was the job for me!

For five months I worked morning, noon, and night. I met with leaders of local teacher groups. I coordinated campaign efforts with other labor unions. I canvassed the streets of King and Snohomish Counties. I smiled through fundraisers and "Meet and Greets." I encouraged skeptical teachers about the need to be involved in state and national politics, about the impact of state and national legislation on their life as a classroom teacher. I did my darndest to convince them of the need to support candidates who, in turn, promised to support education. I promoted the WEA's legislative agenda wherever and whenever possible. The work was exhausting, but I really was thrilled.

In November *The Seattle Times* headline read, "Landslide Victory for Reagan." I was stunned. Almost all of our endorsements had been for Democratic candidates, but it was Ronald Reagan's commitment to "Make America Great Again" that had gotten the country's endorsement. The Republican sweep that began in the east had moved west from Boston to Seattle. I'd been feisty enough to believe that our carefully planned and orchestrated campaign efforts would prove victorious at the day's end, but I'd underestimated the public's sentiment.

I was no longer thrilled.

With each new count and concession speech, I'd watched the wheels come off my own political ambitions. Later in the week when the WEA regrouped on its electoral losses, the final results were in and my job as a campaign organizer was finished. Imagine my disappointment. I'd expected to use my campaign experience to move up in the political world. I'd expected to have my choice of political staff positions. I'd not expected to be part of so many losing efforts. I'd not expected my calls to go unanswered as Democratic friends and associates regrouped on their own political futures. Imagine my frustration. My dreams had vanished with the Republican Party's own carefully planned and orchestrated efforts. And now my turbo-charged ego had hit gravel on what would become a rough stretch in my career journey. Imagine my dismay.

Now I needed to find a new job for the second time in just months. Ready to forge ahead, I considered lobbying. I thought about working for the state legislature or Congress. My parents questioned my decision to continue in politics at all. They saw a bigger and, in many respects, more accurate picture of all things political. They questioned the long days, the huge expectations, the unrelenting schedule. They questioned the role of teachers in politics. Did the union really need a twenty-five-year old lobbyist in the state capital? In Washington, D.C? Did teachers really need to be supporting specific candidates? Did education issues trump all other considerations when voting for someone? When deciding an initiative? They also questioned my interest in lobbying after teaching only four years. Could I really speak with intelligence and authority about life in a classroom? Did I really understand the needs of a teacher? The needs of the teaching system?

My parents cast my career aspirations in a harsh light. Unemployed and uncertain, I'd wanted support and encouragement, not an interrogation of my motives, not a critical analysis of the political system. I felt their distrust of politics unwarranted, their concern about "those darn Democrats" unjustified. In my setback, I'd needed Mom and Dad to be excited for me, to encourage me. Perhaps they'd let me move home for a short time. In the end I got one out of three: they let me move home.

Too busy defending my career choice, I never asked myself whether my parents might be right—at least on some level. Too busy soothing a deflated ego, I hadn't asked for their input. And still not sure how to include God in my plans, I pressed onward, never slowing down, never stopping. I was going to find that perfect job, but I was going to find that perfect job on my own.

Two months later I became an aide for the state's Senate Democratic Caucus. But no sooner had I arranged my desk and found the cafeteria, than a Democratic senator switched to the Republican Party. As a result, the Democrats lost several leadership positions and I lost my "perfect" job. I could only shake my head and wonder how I'd spin my newly acquired unemployment status for Mom and Dad.

Before leaving the capitol building, a former colleague from the WEA called. Steve knew about the Senate upheaval and wanted to hire me back as a lobbyist and political organizer. I jumped at the chance to begin anew—again. With a sigh of relief, I thought about what I'd be able to tell Mom and Dad.

What I didn't realize? That becoming a lobbyist would prove to be another terrible decision. One occasion found me so focused on my upcoming testimony before a senate committee that I missed the fact the bill had been pulled from consideration days earlier. On another occasion, a labor leader got so frustrated with my misunderstanding of an issue that he finally shouted, "You don't know what you're talking about!" He was right. I didn't. But I looked good. I was wearing a gray pinstriped suit, paired with a crisp white blouse and black, three-inch heels. I carried a professional, yet stylish, briefcase and wore just a touch of perfume.

A defining moment. I thought I'd prepared in all the right ways, only to realize I'd focused on all the wrong stuff. The incident was humbling. The criticism stung. The situation reinforced my parents' doubts, doubts that had now become my own. Driving home at the end of another very bad day, I heard myself repeat the words first spoken aloud in an elementary school classroom, "Dear God, what I am doing here?"

I couldn't bear the thought of having to find yet another job. Since I'd left teaching, I'd had three jobs in less than twelve months. In some ways I felt like that teenager who'd careened through the intersection years earlier. Dad's sigh had left me feeling like a disappointment and a failure. Ten years later, I'd feel the same. Not only had I missed the STOP sign with Dad, but I'd also missed God's STOP sign in my professional life. My heavenly Father had needed me to slow down and stop before making career turns, but I'd never bothered to take my foot off the gas. I'd hit the gravel three times, and if I didn't find the brakes soon, I was destined to damage more than truck paint. I needed to stop and get direction, and I needed to get that direction from God.

Staring at a Red Sea of career possibilities, my plea was simple: Now what? Finally I'd come to a complete stop. And in the quiet that came with waiting, I let God speak. I let God direct. I let God move me to put together a resume.

It wasn't the best. My confusion and self-doubts surfaced in a twenty-four-page door-stopper, complete with Table of Contents and sections for Personal Data, Education, Employment History, Leadership Experience, Organizational Experience, and References and Recommendations. Not sure of my marketable skills, I relied on the praises of co-workers and political associates to make me sound professional and worth hiring. The document included letters of recommendation from every last political contact I had, yet nowhere did it say what I might like to do or where I might like to go next.

God's able to work with our imperfections.

Fortunately, God's able to work with our imperfections. He doesn't need prize-winning, well-thought-out attempts at life. He just needs our attention and a willingness to follow direction. In my case, He also needed the attention of Mom and Dad who got the attention of Aunt Lorretta and her husband, Uncle Bob. They had me come into their office where they talked to me about joining their regional brokerage firm. They owned a financial services company in Renton, Washington, and asked me to serve as a liaison between their home office staff and financial advisors. I questioned the offer. I reminded them that I'd taught elementary addition and subtraction, not college economics. They reminded me that I seemed to work well with people. The Red Sea parted. I accepted the job, relieved to know that somewhere within all the verbiage of a twenty-four-page tome they'd found a marketable skill.

Reflecting on my career frustrations, I'd not expected to be forced from the political fast lane by a national referendum. I'd certainly missed the cautionary signs as I sped *into* teaching, but I'd also overlooked the cautionary signs as I sped *out* of teaching. I chose to ignore what should've been obvious. Politics wasn't going to give me the stability I needed: too much uncertainty, too little control, too many promises, too many disappointments, some winners, many losers. Politics wasn't going to promote personal health and well-being: too much coffee, too many cigarettes, long days, longer nights, way too much alcohol. Politics wasn't going to support a young woman's desire to settle down with her boyfriend of eight years. I really wanted to marry Kurt, my college love who was now a history teacher and a high school coach. We hadn't really talked about marriage, but with my life unsettled and chaotic, we never would.

Looking back, a high school photo is telling. I'd served as a page for the Washington State Senate my junior year. Standing with Senator Ted Bottiger, the two of us look like All-American public servants, but the photographer's angle caught us in front of the wrong desk. Our picture-perfect smiles were snapped in front of someone else's nameplate. I'd been caught in the wrong place at the right time. Nine years later I'd feel the same.

Traveling from job to job, I'd never expected to be standing on the shores of my own Red Sea. After pitching headlong into murky career waters, I'd finally surfaced and connected with my aunt and uncle. Hearing my pleas for help, they'd invited me to move forward with them and then they'd parted the waters with words of encouragement and a paycheck. Like Moses had done for the Israelites, they'd held their own version of a walking stick over the sea, leading me to the opposite shore on dry land, promise and possibility awaiting me.

God directed me to a financial side street, but only after I'd come to complete stop. God directed me to relatives who'd not only seen marketable skills in my resume, but seen possibilities in me. They'd believed in me at a time when I didn't. They'd been excited to work with me at a time when I wasn't. They'd seen competence and capability when I'd felt like a failure. They'd also offered me job security. No more ballot-box decisions. No more political antics.

Finally I'd found life's brakes and slowed. Coming to a complete stop at the end of an exit ramp off I-405, I turned into Renton, a city with the slogan, "Renton. Ahead of the Curve." Had I not stopped, I would've missed the curve, no doubt landing in gravel yet again. Back in 1981, finance was a curve in the road I hadn't seen coming, dry ground I hadn't expected, God's direction I'd needed.

Rest Area

1. Any times when you've "hit gravel" in your personal life?

2. Have you ever prepared in all the right ways only to learn you focused on all the wrong stuff?

3. How do you include God in big decisions?

4. How has God worked with your imperfections?

5. How are you able to distinguish God's direction from your own?

Turn Right

That evening a lot of quails came and landed everywhere in the camp, and the next morning dew covered the ground. After the dew was gone, the desert was covered with thin flakes that looked like frost. The people had never seen anything like this, and they started asking each other, "What is it?"

Moses answered, "This is the bread that the LORD has given you to eat. And he orders you to gather about two quarts for each person in your family—that should be more than enough."

They did as they were told. Some gathered more and some gathered less, according to their needs, and none was left over.

—Exodus 16:13-18 (CEV)

Chapter 4

"Why can't we talk about it now?"

"Kurt, why are we turning?"

"I'm going back to the highway."

My husband and I were in Palm Springs on our way to get my favorite coffee drink, a grande-no whip-iced mocha that I had to have now, right now.

"No, just keep going straight," I directed. "Follow the main drag into town."

Kurt kept going straight. He knew it didn't matter how we got to the coffee shop. He was enjoying a beautiful sunny morning in the desert, glad to be with his wife in a rented red convertible, top down. I'd chosen to focus on our destination, taking it upon myself to micromanage our drive block by block, mile by mile.

"Go straight and turn left at the light."

"Now keep going until you get to Indian Canyon."

"Turn right. Here!"

"See that light up ahead? Turn left. Oh, sorry! It's a one-way street. What about the next left?"

Kurt followed each command. When we finally parked the car several minutes later, I thought to myself, really?

Really. I'd been so focused on our destination that I'd missed the joy of a beautiful sunny morning in the desert. I'd missed the fun of a rented red convertible with the top down. I'd missed the pleasure of my husband's company. Remembering the adage, "my way or the highway," I'd made it my way the entire way.

My way or the highway. Even though I'd never spoken the words out loud, the tone in my voice certainly put that morning's message in ALL CAPS. Five words that have often characterized my response to life. Five words of bold type that have highlighted my self-centeredness. Five words that have underscored my lack of appreciation and gratitude, that have *italicized* a mistaken belief that I *always* know best. I'd like to think it was an isolated incident, just one of those days, but it wasn't. I joke about my need to decide everything for everyone, but it's no laughing matter. I've struggled again and again to accept other points of view, other ways of doing things, other ideas about what might be best. And a bigger concern should be my insistence on micromanaging God. I shudder to think the number of times I've told Him, "No, just keep going straight!" He's heard the bold, underscored, italicized, all-caps edge in my voice while I've navigated that bigger journey through life. He knows the difficulty I've had accepting His guidance. He knows the number of times I've "suggested" how best to proceed. He knows how little I've appreciated what is, how often I've focused on what I think can be, needs to be, should be. He saw it in my relationship with Kurt.

Kurt and I married eight years, six months, and three days after meeting at PLU. I'd expected to date through college and marry shortly after graduation. Kurt never got the memo. That's not accurate. The poor guy actually got several memos, most in the form of heartfelt cards and letters promising my unwavering love and support, pleading for some kind of commitment, and then threatening to break up should he not reciprocate. Rarely did I give him a choice. Not ready to commit, overwhelmed by unrequited feelings, he broke up with me—again and again and again.

Our break-ups left me devastated. I truly believed I knew exactly how it could be for us, and Kurt was not cooperating. From the beginning he and I were in different places emotionally, not a Venus and Mars difference, more like two faraway galaxies. I exaggerate, but the feelings and angst were real. We'd only been dating weeks when that distance became evident for the first time. Kurt had taken me for a short walk about campus, his intent to make sure we had some kind of an understanding about our new-found relationship.

"Deanna, I don't want you to feel tied down. You're free to date others, you know."

I took Kurt's words to mean that he was freeing me up to date others *if* I wanted, but since I didn't, he was now my guy. I came back to my dorm room giddy with news of our walk together. Remembering that I was dating a football player, my roommate Sheryl called a quick time out and set me straight. "Uh, Deanna, he's not freeing you up. He's telling you that he wants to be free to date others." Ooooh.

I never gave up. I never gave in. Years later when Kurt broached the subject of marriage, I turned the conversation in the "right" direction. Meeting me for dinner while I was working at the WEA, Kurt suggested we talk about marriage after the November elections. I dropped my fork. *What did he say? Did he just use the word "marriage" in a sentence about us? Does he really think I'm too busy to have a bigger talk? I'm not. Seriously, I can make time.*

I looked across the table. Kurt was slicing into his steak, seemingly oblivious to my excitement. He may have wanted to start with a bigger, more conceptual discussion, but I didn't. I wanted specifics. After waiting years to have this conversation, I wanted to get to the point now, right now. I didn't want to wait another three months. My patience lasted less than twenty-four hours.

"Kurt, why can't we talk about it now?"

"Talk about what?"

"Getting married! Why can't we talk about getting married right now?"

"Aren't you busy with the elections? Wouldn't you rather wait until things quiet down a bit?"

"No!"

And so it went until the "No!" in one conversation became a "Yes!" in another. I'd successfully micromanaged the entire discussion. Rather than stop and appreciate the moment, I had us moving straight ahead, insisting on when and where we'd become engaged (dinner that night) and when and where we'd marry (my church the following July). Eleven months later we were husband and wife, Kurt not getting a chance to say much more than "I do."

When we married, Kurt was a teacher and coach at Tolt High School in Carnation, Washington, a small town east of Seattle. Kurt had wanted to get his Master's in School Administration, so we celebrated our first anniversary with a move back to Parkland where I'd grown up, back to PLU where we'd met, back to my father's rental house where Kurt and I had lived at different times as students. The occasion had us stepping back in time while preparing to step forward in our marriage and Kurt's career.

A year later, his studies finished, Kurt accepted a teaching job at Monroe High School. Right turn followed right turn as we made our way to Monroe, seventy miles north of Parkland. When we left the highway and began our drive down Main Street, I shifted uncomfortably in my seat. I felt conflicted. I was glad that Kurt had gotten the job, but I had mixed feelings about our move. Monroe was east of Snohomish where I'd taught previously. During my teaching days, Monroe had been just a little too unsophisticated, a little too hick for my more suburban taste. I frowned remembering that Kurt planned to coach, too. Snohomish was a larger AAA school, but Monroe was smaller and in the AA division. Snohomish also had a history of winning and Monroe didn't. Now after he'd taken a year to get his degree, I had to remind myself that my husband had gainful employment.

But Monroe? *Really? Monroe?*

One week before the start of school, we moved into a small, two-bedroom apartment. Kurt was close to the high school. I was about forty-five minutes from my job at my aunt and uncle's brokerage firm, a commute that had me turning right into Monroe each night, a right turn that just didn't feel quite right. For months I'd wrestled with our relocation to a place I considered east of somewhere in the middle of nowhere. I took the quickest route out of town each morning. I grabbed groceries—out of town. I mailed letters—out of town. I met friends for dinner—out of town.

Our first son, Kyle, was born twelve months after our move. With my baby nestled into a cloth carrier, I finally began to explore the neighborhood, walking to the grocery store, stopping by the post office, grabbing lunch at the bakery. What I discovered was a small, thriving community.

Kurt and I moved into our first home on April Fools' Day, a day of blessings, not practical jokes. After thirty years, I look at the sign above the garage and smile: *The Nowadnicks.* The wood carving is a simple reminder of a trip to the Evergreen State Fair our first year in the house. The sign's too small to be read from the street. You see it walking up the driveway. When giving directions, I refer to the first house on the left as soon as you turn right. The sign's not helpful for finding us. The sign really names the place that's become our home.

While the cedar fence weathered to a silvery gray, we grew as a family. Two years after Kyle's birth, Kevin was born. Together life was full. There were days that felt like nothing went right and days I managed to get the children fed, the clothes washed, and the bills paid. More than once Kurt came home to a frazzled, weary mom crying, "I just want two minutes to myself!" Both boys outgrew naps long before I did. Both boys were given too much Mac & Cheese, sugared cereal, and hotdogs made from unidentifiable meat products. By the time the boys were in high school, I'd given up trying to plan an evening meal together with Kurt coaching, Kevin in soccer, and Kyle running track. Truthfully, I exploited the vagaries of our afternoon and evening schedules to get out of cooking, not one of my unique abilities. Kyle hit the local drive-thru after practice for a whopper of a burger, catsup only, using special coupons created just for him by the restaurant's manager. Remembering Hillary Clinton's book *It Takes a Village*, I had to concur. For me, it took the love and support of my husband and the kindness of Monroe's entire fast food community.

Remembering my attitude when we moved to Monroe, I shake my head. Arriving in town for the first time, I'd been frustrated with the direction married life had taken. Struggling with my need for control, I'd been unappreciative of the opportunities ahead. I'd reacted poorly when learning Kurt and I would be making a couple right turns as we headed north into the next phase of life. To my heavenly co-pilot, I'd whined, "Just keep going straight!"

Jesus asks, "Which of the two did what his father wanted?"

In the Bible Jesus tells a story about a man with two sons. He asked the first to go and work in the vineyard. He refused but later changed his mind and went. The father went to his other son and asked him to do the same. He said he would but then didn't. After telling the story, Jesus asks, "Which of the two did what his father wanted?" Those listening reply, "The first."

During our time of transition, I behaved like the second son. I said and did all the right things, but my heart was crying out, *No!* I wanted to be excited for Kurt and our move, but I also questioned God. *Monroe? Really, Monroe?* I'd had no appreciation for God's direction and the turns He was asking us to make. Yet in the middle of my spiritual pout, God had responded with "manna from heaven," one whopper of a life, blessings only.

After safely crossing the Red Sea, God had also turned the Israelites right, leading them south through the Sinai Peninsula. They were now in the middle on a long and arduous trek, the excitement of their escape from Egypt behind them, the magnitude of their journey looming larger and larger. This was no cruise through the desert with the top down. Moses was not deciding between one highway or another. Familiar with the area, the people had to have known that they were taking a longer, more circuitous route to the Promised Land, wherever that was. Initially they'd been more relieved than concerned. They rejoiced. They praised God. Their time of slavery was behind them. But then came moments of alarm. The desert was before them. Fear and frustration overtook them.

They cried. "If only we had stayed in Egypt."

They railed. "At least we had meat back in Egypt."

They complained. "In Egypt we were able to eat all that we wanted."

They panicked. "Here in the desert, we're going to starve!"

And God responded in love and faithfulness. "At twilight you will have meat and in the morning you will be filled with bread. Know that I am the Lord your God."

Manna and quail. God's people were given bread in the form of white flakes like frost on the ground. They were also given meat. Carbs and protein! Not only had God led them, but He'd provided for their daily needs.

When we first moved to Monroe, I'd clung to a past that existed elsewhere. I'd railed and complained. After Kyle was born, I began to explore and discover the neighborhood. I learned to appreciate life in a small, thriving community. God had led us to a special place and then given us "manna and quail," food that sustained us physically and spiritually. I'd asked God to go in another direction, but God had turned us right, right where we all needed to be.

My need to micromanage life had been a mistaken belief that I knew best. My attitude had shown no appreciation for life's blessings, life's possibilities. On a beautiful sunny morning in the desert, I'd missed the joy of a simple car ride. In Monroe, I didn't.

Monroe. Really, Monroe.

Rest Area

1. Have you ever been so focused on your destination that you've missed the joy of the ride?

2. Have there been times when you've wanted to micromanage God and His plans for you?

3. Where have you needed to turn right in your travels with God?

4. How has God provided you with "manna and quail"?

5. How are you right where you need to be right now?

No U-Turn

On the morning of the third day there was thunder and lightning. A thick cloud covered the mountain, a loud trumpet blast was heard, and everyone in camp trembled with fear. Moses led them out of the camp to meet God, and they stood at the foot of the mountain.

Mount Sinai was covered in smoke because the LORD had come down in a flaming fire. Smoke poured out of the mountain just like a furnace, and the whole mountain shook. The trumpet blew louder and louder. Moses spoke, and God answered him with thunder.

—Exodus 16:13-18 (CEV)

Chapter 5

"I just want to be on recess duty!"

Since leaving the mountain highway, I'd become more and more anxious. A girls' weekend in Truckee, California, had included a day trip to my college roommate's ranch in the Sierra Mountains. Sitting in the backseat of Sheryl's extended cab pickup truck, I bounced over the rocky terrain and watched the road narrow precipitously. I looked down at my cutie-pie denim capris and Lindsey Phillips sandals as dust enveloped the truck. I was not prepared for a day in the mountains. No fiber of my being had ever wanted to commune with nature, yet here I was traveling through ponderosa pines and shallow creek beds, around hairpin turns and rugged switchbacks on my way to some rustic destination in the woods. I didn't have the nerve to ask where I'd be going to the bathroom.

My unease worsened. I didn't mind that our girls' time included a visit with Sheryl's husband. Tim was easygoing, easy company. I just minded that he wanted to take us on a guided tour of the area, suggesting we climb back into the truck shortly after arrival. *Haven't we already been on a little tour of the area?*

"Come on, girls. Let's go see the sights!"

Yes, let's. Minutes later I was gaping out the truck's window, watching the narrow, dusty road give way to a fire trail, a forest byway that hardly seemed wide enough for hikers, let alone emergency vehicles and our over-sized six-wheeler. Staring in disbelief at the steep drop-off to my right, I could no longer make small talk about the scenery. I got right to the point, "Tim, it's a long way down."

He chuckled.

"Tim, how will we get back down?"

He chuckled again.

"Tim, how *will* we get back down?"

Hearing the anxiety in my voice, Tim teased, "Ha. Ha. I'll just back up."

Hearing the anxiety in my *own* voice, I prayed. *"God, I know You're really busy. I know You have a zillion things way more important right now, but I need to get out of here!"*

Hugging the side of the mountain, trying to navigate sunbaked ruts of compacted dirt, Tim drove on, the truck lurching ahead. My head whipped back and forth as we lunged over fallen tree limbs and forest debris. I'd needed no divine revelation to know there was no turning around, no backing up. Until we reached the top, we had to keep going, higher and higher. I had to hope the trail would support a heavyweight pickup, that the trail would be wide enough for the truck's dual rear wheels, that my nauseousness would pass. And then the answer to prayer: the trail widened, the sun broke through the trees, and a small grassy area opened before us. We'd made it!

Getting out of the truck, I walked cautiously to the edge of the road and found myself staring at a stunningly beautiful landscape, a sparkling blue lake below, emerald green hillsides surrounding me. My distress forgotten, I marveled at the panoramic glory of God's creation. The Sunday before, I'd played Ron Kenoly's hymn "Majesty" on my violin. Rarely do I think about a song's words. I'm usually more focused on the key signature and beats per measure than rhyming verses and a repeated chorus, but now I smiled, remembering the words:

> So exalt
> Lift up on high
> The name of Jesus
> Magnify
> Come glorify
> Christ Jesus the King.

My heart soaring, I stood on top of the hill in awe of the spectacular view, God's magnificence shining brightly in the summer sun. Tim was right. I'd needed to see the sights.

What Tim and I hadn't known was that I'd really needed this moment above the trees to look inside my heart. I'd needed time for spiritual reflection. My whimpered plea for help had been answered, but not in the way I'd expected. God had responded to my self-indulgent request for escape with a beautiful reminder of His majesty. Minutes before I'd been uncomfortable, my pants a little dusty, my stomach a little upset. Now I stood before an unfolding vista. I may not have wanted to commune with nature, but I'd certainly needed to commune with the all-knowing, all-powerful God Who'd created it.

Too often I've treated God like a glorified tour guide. I've decided where I'd like to go and then boarded God's luxury motor coach, expecting a grand adventure with a climate-controlled interior, reclining seat, adjustable foot rest, tinted windows for a picturesque view, and heavy-duty shocks for a smooth ride. I tend to enjoy my time with God as long as He takes me where I want to go, but when He's taken me places that are a little uncomfortable—a little steep and dusty, spiritually speaking—I've developed a short-sighted habit of looking at the narrow road and prayerfully asking God to get me back to something more comfortable. When Jesus refers to the "narrow road leading to life" (Matthew 7:14), my inclination is to think of easier, alternative routes, especially when navigating my professional life.

After working nine years at my aunt and uncle's brokerage firm, I decided to make one more career change. Yes, *one more!* My older son, Kyle, was about to start kindergarten. Thinking about school for him got me thinking about school for me. Despite the difficulties I'd had before, I considered teaching part-time. I told myself I could have summers with my two young sons. I could put my daily commute behind me. I could get medical and dental insurance, a pension.

Ready to charge back into teaching, I resigned from the firm. A week later I got a call from Jeffrey Ross, a financial advisor I'd known many years. His practice, The Planner's Edge, was growing, and he needed office help. He offered me a job as his assistant, but I declined. Remembering Kyle's kindergarten schedule, I added, "Jeffrey, you're used to having someone full-time. I only want to work half days."

A week later Jeffrey called back, insisting he could make the job work part-time. I was flattered, but declined. "Jeffrey, I need to be able to drop Kyle off in the morning and pick him up in the afternoon. I only want to work school hours and school days."

A week later Jeffrey called back again, this time convinced he could make the job work between 9:30 a.m. and 2:30 p.m. Again I was flattered. Again I declined. "Jeffrey, you can't pay me what I'll make teaching," an interesting observation since teachers aren't known for their exorbitant salaries. Jeffrey asked for specifics on teacher pay and benefits, offering to see what he could do. He promised to get right back to me.

While Jeffrey was doing the math, I interviewed with two school districts, Snohomish where I'd taught previously and Monroe where I lived now. Both districts thought they might have a position but neither could make an offer until later in the summer, most likely September when enrollment numbers were known.

As promised, Jeffrey called back with his own offer that was the salaried equivalent of a part-time teaching position. Reminding me that he'd accommodated all my objections, he asked once again that I please consider the job. "You can even 'teach' in your role as my assistant," he cajoled.

Kurt also thought it was time for me to consider Jeffrey's proposal. "Do you realize what he's offering you?" A teacher himself, Kurt knew the demands of the classroom. He also knew his wife. "You weren't happy teaching!"

The next morning I called Jeffrey and told him, "I'll do it. I'll take the job."

A couple weeks later on a memorable September morning, I dropped Kyle off at school and headed into the office, crying the entire way. I'd just learned that Snohomish had a position at my former school and Monroe had a position at Kyle's, just two blocks from home. I was heartbroken—and confused. Still stuck on the idea of returning to the classroom, I couldn't put my new job in perspective. Jeffrey had given me a job that would provide wonderful opportunities as a professional and treasured moments as a mom. But that morning in the car, I saw no wonder, no treasure. All I saw was the trading of one commute for another, still no medical and dental insurance, no pension. I wanted to stomp on the brakes and head back to school, but there was no turning around.

God had to have been shaking his head. After begging Him to get me out of the classroom years earlier, I'd been pleading to get back into a new classroom. Now I was having a spiritual breakdown right there on the freeway and what Oprah would've called "an ugly cry."

"I just want to be on recess duty!" I wailed. Gripping the steering wheel, I put my exasperation into words. More tears followed. I was a wreck emotionally and professionally, troubled by an occupational schizophrenia, one minute ready to look ahead at the possibilities, the next minute clinging to an unsatisfying past. My tears made no sense. God had gotten me through a personal Red Sea when I'd left teaching. He'd led me safely to the opposite shore when I'd gone to work for my aunt and uncle. Now I felt like I was being pulled along a narrow wilderness trail, and I wanted no part of the adventure. I wanted to turn back, but I felt like God was ignoring my discomfort, just as Tim would do years later.

So far my career changes had marked times of disappointment, not times of discovery, not feelings of satisfaction and accomplishment. My identity had become overshadowed by unsatisfying, ill-fitting work and jobs I didn't like or couldn't have. Driving to my new job with Jeffrey, I'd been racked by cries of frustration, my outburst about recess duty indicative of my confusion. I'd hated recess duty. A professional step backward made little sense and again I faced the question: if not a teacher, what? My career had taken so many unexpected turns. Now I just wanted to know what I was going to be when I grew up.

I recently had coffee with a wonderful friend from church. Michol had just started meeting with a professional career coach. In preparation for her first session, she'd made a set of cards. On one side she'd identified her many roles: wife, mother, daughter, business owner, community leader, eight in all. On the flipsides she'd listed the various responsibilities of each, a list that had evolved over time and would continue to do so. I left the coffee shop wondering about the various aspects of my own professional identity, especially my difficulty with change. My roles had evolved, too, but rather than embrace the changes, I'd wanted to put on the brakes. I'd wanted to make a U-turn.

The Israelites had wanted to make a U-turn, too. After escaping from brutal Egyptian slavery, their gratefulness had been short-lived. As the desert grew hotter, their thankfulness and praise cooled. Traveling in directions not expected, they reacted in anger and frustration. Listening to their complaints, it's easy to think, *People! You've just been freed from slavery. Why are you whining? Why do you keep asking to turn back?* How had the Israelites' hearts gotten so hard? How had they forgotten God's faithfulness? His guidance? Pillars of smoke and fire had led them day and night. Manna and quail had sustained them morning and evening. Yet still they'd grumbled.

"Why are we here?"

"What are we supposed to drink?"

"Why in God's name were we brought out of Egypt to die with our children in the desert?"

Why couldn't the Israelites see God's blessings? Why did they keep asking to return to a place of pain and suffering? Why couldn't they accept their new identity as a free people? Why did they cling to a captive past? To lives of enslavement? Why couldn't they just let go and let God continue directing them?

And what about me? Why couldn't I accept a new identity apart from teaching? Why was I clinging to an unsatisfying past? Why couldn't I just let go and let God continue directing me?

God heard the bitter grumblings of the Israelites, and when He'd had enough, He roared from the mountain top, silencing His critics with thunder, lightning, and fire. He let everyone know that it was time for them to let go of the past and accept their new identity as His people. Sobbing on my way into a new office, I'd also needed to let go of the past. I'd needed to take hold of a new identity, remembering that God had been faithfully caring for me throughout my own times of transition.

I find it easy to think of "letting go and letting God" as overly simplistic bumper-sticker theology. The phrase actually comes from the Keswick Movement that began in Keswick, England in 1885. The movement emphasized not only the blessing of our salvation, but the glory that comes with our surrender to God's will. In other words, if we want to experience God's glory, be it thunder, a beautiful vista, or a new opportunity in life, we have to *let go* of the past *and let God* show us the future. In life there are no U-turns.

Personally I find the idea of letting go and letting God redefine me a little unsettling. If pressed, I'd have to confess that I'd rather be sitting in the front seat of God's luxury motor coach asking that my will be done, reinforcing who I believe myself to be. Rather than look to God, it's been easier to whine about both petty inconveniences and major life changes. I bemoan what *has been* without appreciating what *is to come*. During my girls' weekend in Truckee, after we'd gotten back down off the mountain, the lovely vista a memory, I bought a wall plaque that read: "You can't start the next chapter of your life if you keep reading the last one." At the time I thought it was apropos inspiration for writer's block, but the words were better instructions for a "career block."

> God reminds us that He is God, that He will lead us, that
> He will teach us His will and His way.

Perhaps the Israelites had had trouble starting the next chapter in their life, because they'd kept rereading the last one, too. It's easy to do when we're going through personal and professional transformations. But then God's glory shakes the earth and quiets us—on mountains and in life. God reminds us that He is God, that He will lead us, that He will teach us His will and His way. Granted, it's not always the smoothest ride. In my case, God continued to hear some crying and complaining, a little grumbling, stuck as I was reading and rereading the last chapter, remembering who I was, not who I could be. But finally the time came when I actually opened the pages to the next chapter, the one that redefined me not as a teacher (my past) but as Jeffrey's assistant (my future).

Jeffrey and I have now been together twenty-six years. He's taught me a lot. Jeffrey's both book-smart and street-smart. He knows Wall Street and Main Street. He knows investments and investing principles. He knows what questions to ask our clients. He manages serious money seriously. Today I'm his Client Services Specialist which means that I get to micromanage all the moving pieces of his clients' financial strategies. May I repeat that? I *get* to micromanage.

Remembering the past, it's easy to lose sight of God's bigger picture for tomorrow. It's easy to get focused on the dust, the heat, immediate anxieties. At times God's had to take me "to see the sights." At times God's had to get my attention in dramatic ways. In the Sierras, I'd had no real appreciation for where I was until I'd gotten above the trees and looked around. In life, I'd had no real appreciation for my opportunity with Jeffrey until I'd gotten well into my career and looked back.

No U-turns. Once we let God, we're able to let go. Once we let go and let God, we're able to move forward into our next chapter with confidence and joy, without fear and hesitation. The story's magnificent. So is the view.

Rest Area

1. Has there been a time when you've wanted to make a U-turn in your personal life? Your professional life?
2. Has God ever needed to get your attention with "thunder and fire"?
3. How have you let go and let God?
4. What's being written in the next chapter of your own life?
5. How are you able to give God glory?

Milepost

God said to the people of Israel:

I am the LORD your God, the one who brought you
    out of Egypt where you were slaves.
Do not worship any god except me.
Do not make idols that look like anything in the sky or
    on earth or in the ocean under the earth.
Do not misuse my name.
Remember that the Sabbath Day belongs to me.
Respect your father and mother, and you will live a
    long time in the and I am giving you.
Do not murder.
Be faithful in marriage.
Do not steal.
Do not tell lies about others.
Do not want anything that belongs to someone else.
                    —Exodus 20:1-4, 7-8, 12-17 (CEV)

Chapter 6

"Hey, where's my suitcase?"

Mirrors adjusted? Check. Seat adjusted? Check. Doors locked? Gas? Check. Pulling my seatbelt snug, I smile, remembering the to-do list that's been with me since high school Driver's Ed class. Today I just push Button #1 on the driver's side door and wait while the car responds to my personalized settings. In seconds the seat eases up, mirrors fan out, doors lock. I'm ready.

Surrounded by so much automation, I'd like to think I've become a better driver, but that's not the case. Not long ago, I picked up my younger son, Kevin, for our weekly lunch date. Finding an open spot on California Avenue in West Seattle, I parked a block away from our favorite Asian restaurant. After eating, Kevin and I walked back toward the car and noticed the lights were on. "It's because the car's running, Mom." In a calm, matter-of-fact tone, Kevin stated the obvious. I'd parked and left the car running while we ate, the keyless-entry, keyless-ignition key fob in the front seat's cup holder. I'd unwittingly left my car idling while we'd worked our way through plates of beef teriyaki and spicy chicken.

Who does that? Who leaves their car running while parked on a busy street? My car has everything to make driving easier. Messages pop up when the oil needs changing, when the fuel is low, when a tire needs air. If I'm within five miles of a Starbucks, I'll know. My seat warms in the winter and cools in the summer. The radio alternates between AM, FM, and satellite. I can listen to replays of Oprah. I can sing along to the '60s, '70s, and '80s. *The car even beeps when it's left running!* But here's the issue: without that driving to-do list, I struggle to stay focused on the tasks at hand, and without certain tasks forcing me to pay attention, I don't.

No, I just don't pay attention. My West Seattle lapse in judgment might be blamed on a mother's excitement to see her son. But other lapses are another issue. Knowing I don't have to worry about when to change the oil, I worry about the latte in my right hand. I spend more time fussing over the radio's playlist than executing a lane change. And my driving suffers. Rarely am I fully engaged in the task at hand. Shrinking into my cooled, black leather bucket seats, I resolve to change, a resolution that's invariably broken before I've backed out of my driveway.

And then there's another problem: some lists are helpful, but others can turn into self-centered iterations of things I have to do, need to do, want to do—to the exclusion of anyone or anything else. The lists themselves aren't the problem. We all create and use lists—grocery lists, Christmas lists, lists of people, places, and things. Lists are important for organizing to-do's, for prioritizing next steps and accomplishing key tasks, for doing our best, being our best. *Lists can help keep us drivers safe for goodness sakes!* But some of my lists can become exacting requirements for getting through the day, for getting through anything. Requests become demands. Tasks become chores. Responsibilities become onerous undertakings. Lists become a "Gotcha!" tally of things not done and missing. Yes, missing. For me, a highway milepost would mark a turning point in my organizational acumen.

For Christmas one year, our family traveled to Idaho. Kurt and our two sons expected to ski and snowboard. I planned to relax with my knitting and a good book. Our adventure started with the usual checklist of things to do, items to pack. With the car loaded, we began a seven-hour trek that took us across the Cascade Mountains, through Eastern Washington, and into Idaho. At Coeur D'Alene, we left Interstate 90, and for the next ten miles, we inched our way through steep terrain and compact snow and ice. Our travels might have been picturesque had it not been so dark, the road so treacherous. We struggled to see, searching in vain for directional signs, all buried in snow banks lining the road.

When we finally arrived at our destination, I kicked the snow from my shoes and slumped onto the couch of our rented condo, relieved to have the white-knuckle drive behind us. The car unloaded, I looked around the room and asked, "Hey, where's my suitcase?"

No response. The uncomfortable quiet said it all. While barking orders during our preparations to leave, I'd neglected to direct anyone's attention to my suitcase, packed and ready to go in our bedroom. Kurt and the boys couldn't have guessed, nor would they have dared to suggest, that I might have forgotten anything. In the hours preceding our departure, I'd been snipping and sniping though a detailed list of travel preparations. Now we were 347 miles from home without my toothbrush, hairspray, and pajamas, no Christmas outfit, no Christmas gifts.

Taking the high road in what could've become a slick and icy stretch in our marital relations, Kurt calmly and quietly said, "I'll go get it. I can be back by morning."

Frustrated and embarrassed, I quickly replied, "I'll go, too. It's my suitcase. It's my fault."

Our sons were young adults, but old enough to know that the road home was going to be fraught with danger, the road conditions being the least of our worries. They opted to stay put and await our return the next day.

Leaving the mountain, I silently fumed. *How did this happen? My suitcase was twice the size of any other bag. How could I have missed it?* Now I just wanted to get home, get some sleep, grab my luggage, and get back to our sons.

Halfway into the return trip, Kurt suggested we grab a hotel room and sleep a little. We could freshen up, perhaps grab a few things before circling back around. "Deanna, why don't we just buy you some PJs? Something nice for Christmas?"

I said nothing.

Feeling hopeful, Kurt went on, "We could get you a toothbrush. They might even have hair stuff at the next truck stop—"

I cut him off with a terse, "I just want to get home."

Kurt drove on. He knew better than to argue with a woman whose frustration might become irrational should he also mention her missing mascara.

At Milepost 45 along I-90, I was startled out of my pout by a loud bang and sideways jolt. We'd blown a tire. It was now near midnight and we were on a dark, deserted, very snowy stretch of highway miles from the suggested hotel room and many more miles from home. Taking the next exit, Kurt parked on the side of the ramp, and then kneeling in roadside slush, he began the miserable task of changing the tire.

He never said a word. Kurt had every right to remind me that I was the one to forget the suitcase, that I was the one who'd asked to accompany him, that I was the one who'd insisted on driving when he'd wanted to rest. He never asked about my checklist, never referred back to our moments before leaving. In love and kindness, he changed the tire and got us home. Without any reference to personal shortcomings, he picked up my suitcase and drove us back to Idaho for a wonderful week as a family.

He never said a word. On a miserable night while holding the flashlight, I'd illuminated not just a flat tire, but a lesson in managing life's to-do's and an even bigger lesson in love and kindness. Getting ready for our week away, we'd both put together lists of things to be done. Side-by-side our lists were similar. Clothes washed? Check. Mail stopped? Check. Tire chains? Gas? Check. All were important. The difference between our lists? I'd made our preparations all about me. "I'm washing clothes now. If I don't have your jeans in ten minutes..." Kurt had made our preparations all about us. "Kyle, would you grab the bags in the living room? Kevin, would you bring me the snowboarding gear?" To anyone listening, we sounded exactly the same, like any two parents corralling teenage boys for a family vacation, trying to ensure an orderly departure. I couldn't see the difference until we'd blown a tire. Squinting into the blowing snow,

I looked around for a sign. Milepost 45 marked not only miles traveled, but a moment of love, a place of kindness.

When the Israelites left Egypt, they'd had no time to work through checklists. Pharaoh had said, "Go!" and they'd gone. Six hundred thousand men along with women and children, fled with their flocks and herds. In the wilderness three months later, God spoke to Moses on Mount Sinai. In a dramatic moment of thunder and lightning, trumpets and smoke, God spelled out a master to-do list, rules for right living that we call the Ten Commandments. On stone tablets in clear, concise language, God told Moses how the Israelites were to love Him and to love others. Mount Sinai would become a milepost in their own travels with God, a turning point in their relationship with Him.

God waited more than three months before giving Moses the Ten Commandments. Rather than start their travels with lists of things to do, He'd first gotten them through the Red Sea. Then He'd nourished them with manna and quail and made sure they'd had water to drink. When they'd grumbled and complained, He'd responded in love and kindness. He'd had every right to say, "Hey, wait! You're the ones who'd wanted out of slavery. You're the ones who'd pleaded day in and day out for freedom. You're the ones who'd asked for food, for water." Instead God had responded with love and kindness. And then on a mountain top, God had given them instructions on how to love Him and each other. Love and kindness.

Pulling my spiritual seatbelt snug, I think back on my travels with God. Too many times I'd snipped and sniped my way through God's commandments, treating them like some kind of "Top 10" checklist. Don't swear. Yep. Go to church. Yep. Don't covet. Needs improvement. Sometimes I've even had the audacity to respond "Does Not Apply." But then I'm stopped by the spirit of God's law. Have I hurt someone's reputation with gossip? Have I robbed the boss of time? Have I treated Kurt with the love and kindness he deserves?

The Ten Commandments provide a guide for right living, a guide that has inspired and directed countless generations, five

"You shall" and five "You shall not" rules. Interestingly, while all provide spiritual direction, there is nothing about packing for long trips, nothing about time with a book and knitting. Pulling my spiritual seatbelt even tighter, I'm humbled. God must have known that if I'm right in my relationship with Him and others, I'll be personally just fine. And should I "forget my suitcase" after a self-centered afternoon of preparations, God will meet me with love and kindness. Should I get distracted and "leave the keys in the ignition," God will get me refocused with love and kindness. And should I insist on grumbling and complaining, God will redirect me with love and kindness—after shining the light on my attitude.

Jesus was a frequent target for the scorn and admonition of religious leaders. He didn't always follow the rules the way they thought he should. They'd extracted the love from God's commands and made His laws into "Gotcha!" moments. Again and again Jesus had to remind them of the spirit of the law, the "heart" of the law, the love.

> "The loudest messages come in the silence."
> —Kurt Latimore

I do. Our wedding vows included two small words, short answers to the biggest question Kurt and I had ever been asked. They came after that split-second quiet, that hold-your-breath interlude when everyone wonders if he and she will say yes, if either will change their mind. Years later, I learned that it's not the quiet that can be measured in seconds that counts, but the quiet measured in the length of a tire change, in the quiet of a loving heart on a miserably cold and snowy night. Hearing my story, my friend Kurt Latimore said, "The loudest messages come in the silence."

Milepost 45—miles traveled and a lesson in love and kindness.

Rest Area

1. Have you ever inadvertently left the car running? Forgotten a suitcase?
2. In your travels with God, has there been a turning point? A special milestone?
3. How can you keep from treating the Ten Commandments like a master to-do list?
4. How do you balance what's best for you with what's best for those around you?
5. What messages have you been able to hear in the quiet?

Wrong Way

Listen, Israel! The LORD our God is the only true God! So love the LORD your God with all your heart, soul, and strength. Memorize his laws and tell them to your children over and over again. Talk about them all the time, whether you're at home or walking along the road or going to bed at night, or getting up in the morning. Write down copies and tie them to your wrists and foreheads to help you obey them. Write these laws on the door frames of your houses and on your town gates.

—Moses, in Deuteronomy 6:4-9 (CEV)

Chapter 7

"Please, God, no! Please, God, no!"

Good grief! Really? Hey, bud, you're going the wrong way! Who drives through a coffee stand like that? Idling face to face in front of the offending driver, I glanced at the clock on my dashboard: 8:10. Ugh! I'd planned to be at church by 8:00 to practice my violin before Sunday worship. Already ten minutes late, I zeroed in on the SUV packed with passengers heading somewhere, each awaiting their drink of something.

Are you from out of town? Have you never used an espresso window before? Not wanting to make eye contact with any of them, I looked down, my eyes catching the time, now 8:15. *So how many drinks have you all ordered?* I was going to be so very late.

At last cups began to appear. *Well, look at that! Large sizes of everything! No wonder your order took so long! Oh, great! And paying with a credit card, too. That'll cost me another five minutes!*

At 8:21 the SUV finally—*finally!*—pulled away. The driver and his passengers waved while I looked straight ahead. I had no time for smiles and certainly no patience for wrong-way antics. Pulling up to the window, I placed my order. The barista smiled and replied, "Got it! And guess what? The people in front of you felt badly for driving the wrong way and taking so much time. They paid for your drink!"

"They bought my sixteen-ounce iced mocha?"

"Yes! Pretty nice, huh?"

I looked back over my shoulder at the departing SUV. *You paid for my drink!* Shame rushed over me. I felt ridiculously petty. On a Sunday morning—on my way to church, no less—I'd sat in my car for eleven minutes and berated an errant driver for having the audacity to misuse the drive-thru. I'd taken cheap shots at people I didn't know, people like me who'd just wanted to start their day with a favorite coffee drink. My offensiveness stung.

At church minutes later, I appeared the model of decorum in my white blouse and dark slacks, violin tucked under my chin, bow coaxing notes from the strings. With my iced mocha beside me, the music of hymns reverberated about the sanctuary. No one would have guessed that minutes earlier I'd been a very unattractive example of impatience and self-centeredness.

How could I have been so insufferably intolerant and unkind in my thoughts? And the bigger question? How had my personal life become so detached from my spiritual life? I'd disconnected from God in a way not expected. *I'd* actually been the one traveling the wrong way. *I'd* been the one totally turned around. I'd focused on the inconsequential, the insignificant, the irrelevant. *I didn't have to practice!* More important was my irritation with people who'd gotten in my way, interrupted my schedule, inconvenienced my plans. I'd shown a regrettable lack of faithfulness, not a disconnect from my belief in God, but a disconnect from my walk with Him.

It was not the first time God had found me traveling the wrong way on a Sunday. Years earlier I'd almost ruined Easter in a close encounter with an open mic. At the time I'd been given the honor of sharing a beautiful soliloquy. Instead of a sermon, I'd been asked to tell the story of Mary's walk to the tomb Easter morning. Mary was one of Jesus' friends, the first one to learn of His resurrection. The piece was beautifully written and I was excited to be a part.

I've always loved Easter. Growing up in the church, Easter had been a time of brass anthems, banners, and lilies, lots of lilies. The church of my youth had a bell tower that welcomed us Sunday mornings. A striking wall of stained glass bathed the sanctuary in the first light of day. Side windows colored the aisles in streams of pink and blue. The altar was draped in beautiful paraments, decorative cloths thoughtfully designed and meticulously stitched. A fifteen-foot banner hung from the chancel wall behind the altar. A trumpet fanfare brought us to our feet for "Jesus Christ Is Risen Today," the choir adding harmony to our melody. It was breathtaking. It was majestic. It was glorious.

In Monroe, we had no bell tower, large choir, or brass accompaniment. Still we'd be celebrating Easter in our own grand way, rising in song, sitting in prayer, and standing in recognition of an unfolding miracle. And yes, I got to be a part.

I practiced and practiced and practiced. My one-act performance was expected to give words to the dramatic events of Easter morning, words that would help give meaning to an event that was really beyond comprehension. I wanted to do well. I thought seriously about Mary's wonder, her concern and fear that blessed day. I prayed that I might capture some measure of her thoughts and feelings.

On Easter morning, I walked into the sanctuary as Mary might have walked to the tomb. Wearing a long robe of coarse linen, I approached the altar slowly, trembling with the words she might have said. "It's so dark! Oh, God, where are You?"

Turning toward the congregation, I shared Mary's anguish. "It wasn't supposed to be this way. Jesus said He was the Messiah. He said He would sit on David's throne. David's throne! Instead I watched Him die on a cross. A horrible death on a cross!"

Trembling, I turned back and cried out, "What's this? Where's the stone?" Envisioning the tomb and a robed figure inside, I voiced Mary's surprise and concern. "Where is my Lord? Sir, if you have taken my Lord, please tell me where you have put him?"

Again I looked at the audience, this time moving from face to face, making eye contact before proceeding. In a hushed voice, I marveled, "And then He said my name, 'Mary.' My name! My Lord spoke to me! My Lord spoke to me as I speak to you! My Lord was alive!"

My monologue finished with "He is risen! He is risen indeed!" I left carrying a single lily back down the aisle. The hush in the room was palpable, deep and profound. With each step, I thanked God for the chance to touch His people in a most memorable way.

Outside the sanctuary doors, I handed the flower to my friend Tom and blurted out an expletive as I collapsed into a chair, the stress behind me. Looking up, I saw him shush me with an index finger to his lips. With his other hand, he pointed to my lapel. It was then that I remembered the wireless microphone—still on. My heart pounding, my head ringing, my stomach churning, my eyes began to water. Rather than conclude my dramatic monologue with a sincere "Amen," I'd just cussed into a small mic clipped to my gown. The hush in the small entry room was almost palpable, deep and profound.

Please, God, no. Please, God, no. Please don't let me end this beautiful morning this way! Unable to move, I watched the service continue. No one jerked to attention. No one flashed a quick look at the exit doors. No one gasped into their service bulletin. Could it be that no one had heard?

No one *had* heard. As it turned out, the wireless mic didn't work outside the sanctuary. The service ended with our pastor sharing the benediction, words God had given to Moses for Aaron to use in blessing the people:

The Lord bless you and keep you;
The Lord make His face shine upon you and be
gracious to you;
The Lord turn his face toward you and give you peace.
Numbers 6:24-26 (NIV)

Never had God's words held such meaning for me. God had blessed and kept me at my most undeserving. Wiping away the tears, I caught my breath, a shudder of relief and gratitude engulfing me. I'd exited church the wrong way and a loving, merciful, very understanding God had silenced me. With a heartfelt sigh, I fell back into the chair, knowing this particular Easter I would be celebrating two miracles, one that had saved all of humankind and one that had saved me.

God also silenced Moses after his own lapse in faithfulness. When the Israelites couldn't find water, Moses lost his patience. God had said, "Speak to the rock and it will pour out water." Angry and frustrated with the people's complaints, Moses had raised his arm and cried out, "Here, you rebels!" Then he'd struck the rock and water had gushed out. But Moses had acted the wrong way, and God had been quick to respond. "Because you didn't trust me, you will not enter the Promised Land."

A harsh punishment. But rather than slump into a chair and shout expletives across the Jordan River, Moses had continued preparations for the Israelites' entrance into the Promised Land. Even though he wouldn't be going with them, Moses found words to celebrate a forty-year miracle. In a farewell address that would become the entire book of Deuteronomy, he spoke to the people as they waited on a sandy threshold to their new life. He reminded them of their journey, including those times when they'd gone the wrong way, when they'd been insufferably intolerant, unkind, and whiny. He exhorted them to honor the God Who'd delivered them from slavery, cared for them when they'd been hungry and thirsty, hot and tired, and then led them to the Promised Land. He reminded them of God's faithfulness. No doubt he'd wanted to impress upon them everything they'd learned and experienced. He wanted to make sure they remained faithful in their walk with God. Moses knew they were reaching the end of one journey and about to start a new one. They'd need to stay focused on the one true God—whether at home, walking along the road, going to bed at night, or getting up in the morning.

> Our God keeps His promises—not just to us but to generation after generation to those who love Him and keep His commands."

In what had to have been an impassioned plea, Moses cried out, "Love the Lord your God with all your heart and with all your soul and with all your strength." Moses reminded them, "Our God is a faithful God. Our God keeps His promises—not just to us but to generation after generation to those who love Him and keep His commands."

After my encounter with the open mic, I resolved to stay faithful. I left church that morning renewed and inspired. It didn't last. My patience waned before reaching the parking lot. Steering my two young sons toward the car, I quickly put off any reference to holiday festivities. "I don't want to hear about Easter eggs until we get home. We're having lunch before candy!" Hearing the tone of my voice, I shook my head and started over. "Come on! Let's go see what a rabbit's left at our house."

Loving God with all our heart and soul and strength is a challenge. Lapses plague us. Moses was hot and tired and thirsty. He was at the culmination of a forty-year journey, one that had to have been ending in a crushing disappointment for him personally. I was just impatient and cross, short-sighted and self-centered.

Two embarrassing episodes are nagging reminders of times I've traveled the wrong way—even on Sundays, even in church. Like the Israelites, I've had moments that have gone awry, days that have fallen apart, wonderful efforts that weren't so wonderful. I've experienced stress and fear and pettiness, disconnecting with God when I've needed Him most.

To the Israelites, Moses said, "Listen, Israel! Our God is the only true God!" We travel with a magnificent God, a God Who's promised to be with us at all times, even when we're stressed and fearful, and yes, even when we're petty. We may struggle with faithfulness, but we travel with a God Who's forever faithful, not only on those days when we're traveling the right way, but also on those days when we're traveling the wrong way.

Especially on those days when we're traveling the wrong way.

Rest Area

1. Has your personal life ever become detached from your spiritual life?
2. How do you stay connected to God, day by day, minute by minute, year in and year out?
3. How has God blessed you and kept you?
4. How has God made His face shine on you and been gracious to you?
5. How has God given you peace?

Road Narrows

From the fullness of his grace we have all received one blessing after another. For the law was given to Moses; grace and truth came through Jesus Christ.

—John 1:16-17 (NIV)

Chapter 8

"I wanted to say goodbye."

I didn't know what I'd say. Grandma was dying and Mom had asked me to go and say goodbye. Leaving work, I began the thirty-minute drive to Grandma's nursing home. Goodbye. The word seemed woefully inadequate for the conversation I was about to have with a beloved lady. I'd said the word almost every day of my life—as I skipped out of a room, as I left friends and family, the expectation being that I would return, sometimes sooner, sometimes later. This was more than a goodbye for the evening.

Driving down the interstate, I clung to the right lane, slipping below the speed limit, hoping for a few extra minutes to think, reflect, and find words. I *really* didn't know what I'd say. For someone who talked a lot, who *always* seemed to have something to say, I was actually at a loss for words. I'd often treated conversation too lightly, talking more than necessary whether I had something to say or just thought I did. Grandma used to call me a chatterbox. More than once, she'd taken me out for a walk in the garden when Grandpa had had enough. Grandpa didn't do chatter.

Tonight was really about Grandma, not me, but our memories were bound together. I began to think about afternoon tea parties and summers in a backyard hammock. When she lived across the street, Grandma used to fill a small teapot with cold milk and then arrange brown sugar sandwiches on matching plates. Together we'd sip "tea" from delicate blue and white cups. I don't remember whether her dishes were fine porcelain or five-cent bargains from Woolworth's, but we treated them like exquisite treasures. On warm summer afternoons she'd have Grandpa set up a hammock under the grape arbor. We'd sit in the small shaded enclosure and talk and talk. Years later when she tucked a precious lace hanky into the sleeve of my wedding dress, we smiled in remembrance of beautiful afternoons.

What Grandma never seemed to remember were the times that were not so exquisite, the times my brother came with me and we ended up arguing over who got the hammock, fighting over who got the bigger sandwich, the times she sent us home early because we'd tried her patience and Grandpa's. With every knock on her door came a warm and inviting "Come on in, dearie." Now I'd be knocking on her door one last time.

Arriving at the nursing home, I parked and entered the building. I proceeded down the hallway slowly, finally nearing Grandma's room, still no closer to the words I so desperately wanted for this last chat. Yet before I could reach her bedside, Grandma's cries of anguish greeted me with the difficult truth, "I'm dying! I'm dying!"

With her harsh words echoing off the sterile walls of her room, my own words of love and sadness came in quiet reply. "I know, Grandma, that's why I'm here. I wanted to say goodbye." Expecting to give her comfort, I recoiled with each outcry. Her breathing was shallow, but her desperation resounded with an unforeseen intensity.

My dear grandmother had been "dying" for as long as I could remember. She'd had her first heart attack during our tea party days. Over the years her heart had been supported by a row of carefully arranged, ever increasing, plastic prescription bottles atop her bedroom dresser. She'd been so frail for so long I'd gotten accustomed to thinking about Grandma being "near" death. Now she really was.

And then another gasp, another piercing cry. "I'm dying! I'm dying!"

I looked at Grandma as she fell back on the bed. *Grandma, are you in pain? What's really going on here?* I'd assumed that Grandma was just afraid of that last moment, these last moments, certainly reason enough to cry out. Now I wondered if my God-fearing grandmother was not only terrified of death, but horrified by the spiritual ramifications of death. Perhaps the thought of "meeting her Maker" was just too frightening. Perhaps the thought of that final judgment was more than she could bear.

My God-fearing grandmother. I'd never really talked about God with Grandma. I'd actually been afraid to. I'd always felt that her God was more law than love. Her God seemed to be all rules and no fun. Her God seemed to have heavy, almost oppressive, expectations of obedience that were impossible to attain or maintain, especially for someone like me who had a problem following the rules. Regardless, I'd expected Grandma to have her eyes on the clouds looking for Jesus' outstretched arms. Now it seemed she might have been fearing an angry God ready to condemn and punish her for a lifetime that hadn't measured up. I was startled to think that this kind, gracious lady, my "heart for God" grandmother, might have been so unsure, so anxious, and so afraid.

"Grandma, it's going to be okay." I badly wanted her to know that whatever she faced, she was not alone, that her family surrounded her, but even as I said the words, I knew deep down that her discomfort was not about loneliness and people in the room. I continued, "God loves you very, very, very much. I know He's with you right now. You don't have to be afraid, Grandma. You don't have to worry. You are His own dear child. He did everything He could to make sure you would be with Him forever. Grandma, He gave you Jesus."

"He gave you Jesus." I'd found the words, first a reminder of my love and then a bigger reminder of God's. More significant than saying goodbye had really become a few words of hope and promise. Her road had narrowed. A lifetime had narrowed to a single day, a single place, a single moment in time. Tonight had not only been about Grandma, but even more important, tonight had been about God.

I'd never expected to be walking into what might have been a spiritual crisis for my grandmother. I was only forty-four at the time, old enough to know that our walk with God was more than a stroll in the park, that it could be long and difficult. Thinking about Grandma's journey, I had to wonder if she felt like she was on a metaphorical freeway, six lanes of God's law ahead of her, directional arrows and caution signs every couple miles. Her travels would've been daunting, especially as she neared the end. But that six-lane interstate of rules and regulations, laws and commandments narrows to a single lane marked "Grace," a designated lane in which God meets us with His mercy and forgiveness. Grandma knew she deserved God's judgment. We all do. We all fall short of those many laws given to Moses and given to us. But God leads us to that one lane of grace in which we find Jesus, God's very own son and our very own savior. Jesus' death and resurrection brings us life, even as we lay dying.

Years later I found myself in that same lane of grace with my own father. Both my mom and dad died relatively young: Mom was only sixty-eight; Dad was just seventy. Mom died at Easter; Dad died two and a half years later at Christmas. Their deaths forever changed me, but Dad's death had the most profound effect.

At the time he died, I'd been trying to reach my father for several days. He'd neglected to call Kevin on his sixteenth birthday, not alarming since we'd celebrated days earlier, but still somewhat surprising. I called that weekend. No answer. *Dad, where are you?* Getting no response again Monday morning, I decided to drive to his house, but before I could leave, the phone rang.

"Hello, this is the Pierce County Sheriff's office calling for Deanna Nowadnick."

"This is Deanna."

Something had indeed happened. Dad had missed breakfast with his friend Gene. Since their retirement, they'd met weekly for scrambled eggs and coffee. They used the time together to enjoy each other's company and talk through the world's problems. They groaned over the changes in education and railed against the Democrats in Olympia and Washington, D.C. They bragged about grandchildren. They mourned losses. Never missing their weekly get-togethers, Gene had known immediately that something was wrong when Dad didn't show.

And then the call to me: "We found your father."

The emergency medical personnel said Dad died of a heart attack. More than a matter of semantics, I knew that Dad had actually died of a broken heart. After losing Mom, Dad had lost hope. Mom had been the love of his life, the girl he'd fallen for at first sight some fifty years earlier. He'd seen a tall girl in glasses across the courtyard on their first day of class at Pacific Lutheran College. After learning her name, Dad had announced, "I'm going to marry that girl." And he did—a month after graduation. Never far from that courtyard, Mom and Dad had settled into a modest house, raising me and my brother, David. They enjoyed successful teaching careers and then retired to a life of leisure and travel as members of the AARP.

Learning of Dad's death, I wept in despair. I'd broken my father's heart time after time. For years I'd challenged him and now he was gone. I cried in sorrow. I'd been the bane of his existence for years, a source of sadness and frustration for decades. I also sobbed in relief. After Mom's death, Dad and I had had a chance to regroup, and I'd begun mending a relationship that I'd been shredding for years. Waves of sadness and relief, mourning and an unexpected peace washed over me.

Growing up, I'd often balked at being told what to do. My father had had high expectations, and I'd had high objections. His expectations actually overwhelmed me and were really of no interest to me. I was only five when I came home from school with a neighborhood classmate. Debbie and I walked into the house with our first papers from kindergarten. With my colored picture of a lion placed next to Debbie's, the differences were obvious. She'd stayed within the lines and I hadn't. She'd colored her lion in "lion" colors and I'd chosen bright "non-lion" colors. My father's disapproval was deeply felt. I'd not been scolded, but I'd known immediately that something was wrong. I'd fallen short of expectations I didn't understand and didn't appreciate. I'd had no interest in a "Burnt Orange" and "Raw Sienna" lion on "Forest Green" grass!

And so I rebelled, one small art project beginning a pattern of increasingly dysfunctional behavior. Not knowing how to give voice to my feelings, I grew up challenging Dad about everything, large and small, significant and not. I refused to appreciate a parent trying to parent. The underlying stress and tension colored the fabric of our family. As a teen, I'd mastered the fine art of provocation, which was not so fine. By the time I was a young adult, I had little in common with my father. Dad voted Republican; I voted for anyone who was not. Dad loathed labor unions; I became president of the Snohomish Education Association. Dad despised lobbyists and special interest groups; I lobbied for a special interest group. If he marveled at the beauty of a spring morning, I found the cloud in the sky. Some of our differences were a real divergence in thoughts and feelings, but most were just the defiant responses of a young woman who'd decided she wanted nothing to do with her father and his expectations of her.

My relationship with Dad came into sharp focus after Mom died. After fighting him for decades, I found the will to call a cease-fire and begin what would become a two-year goodbye. Taking the author Anne Lamott at her word, I could either practice being right or practice being kind. With God's help, I was able to practice being kind. What surprised me was how kindness became tolerance, and tolerance became understanding. Understanding became acceptance, and acceptance became love, a messy, imperfect love encased in my own messier version of grace.

> Grace is that narrow lane on life's six-lane interstate,
> that lane in which we travel at the speed of love.

To quote Lamott, "I do not understand the mystery of grace—only that it meets us where we are and does not leave us where it found us." Grace is that narrow lane on life's six-lane interstate, that lane in which we travel at the speed of love. Enjoying long lunches together, I learned to smile when Dad blamed the demise of civil society on "those flaming liberals." He chuckled while I recounted my own parenting fiascos. I was finally able to acknowledge that Dad and I shared a passion for our different beliefs. We shared a deep and abiding love of family. God had indeed met me where I was and not left me where He found me. God and His grace changed my actions, changed my heart, changed me.

Grandma and I had just minutes to say goodbye. Dad and I had months. Moses and the Israelites had all of Deuteronomy. In a goodbye that lasted thirty-four chapters, Moses spoke to the people while they waited on the banks of the Jordan River, ready to cross into the Promised Land. Moses was not going with them, the consequence of his own moment of exasperation and impatience. In a final address, he reminded the people of God's law and how it would prepare and sustain them for new lives in a new land. Again and again he reminded them of the need to be obedient, using the words "obey" and "obedient" fourteen times. He referred to God's commands and the commandments twenty times.

"See! I've taught you God's laws as He commanded. You'll need to follow these laws when you enter the Promised Land."

"You must worship and obey God."

"Love the Lord with all your heart. Obey the commands He's given you."

The word Deuteronomy actually means "repetition of the law." In chapter after chapter Moses restated specific laws and then reminded the Israelites of their need to follow those laws. His words of admonition seem to reinforce Grandma's fear of a hard-hearted, stern, demanding God. I'd often felt the same about Dad. What Grandma may not have appreciated—and what I *certainly* didn't appreciate!—was that some rules actually come bound in love. My father's love was a heartfelt commitment to be the best he could be, expecting his daughter to be the best she could be. God's love also raises the bar for each one of us. We're expected to be the best we can be as His chosen people, but when we fall short, God meets us in a narrow lane of grace. God walked with Moses in that lane of grace, taking him to his final resting place. I believe God met Grandma in that lane of grace, too, as she lay dying in a nursing home. And God definitely met me in that lane of grace at lunch with my father.

In Washington, the Golden Apple Awards recognize educators, programs, and schools making a difference in education. Without exception, winners speak of expecting the best from their students. Maureen David, the former principal of Hudtloff Middle School in

Tacoma, shared a common sentiment, "If you don't expect the best from students, regardless of their background, you are doing them a disservice."

I smile in remembrance of Dad's teaching days. My father had taught at Hudtloff. He, too, had expected excellence. He'd wanted the very best from his special education students, supporting them in every way possible. Dad had also had high expectations of me, a special needs kid in many ways. With God's help, I was finally able to see that Dad's expectations were his way of raising the bar for a daughter he loved and cared about. Seeing a brightly colored lion, I don't think he'd meant to stifle my creativity; I think he'd meant to inspire greatness *as best he could*. Dad was a traditionalist and really wanted me to be more like him, a true-colors kind of gal, a card-carrying Republican. That never changed. What changed was me.

If we're not careful, it's easy to miss the love in which God's law is given. It's easy to get focused on the huge expectations and our huge shortcomings. Without grace, Grandma faced a God of judgment, an angry God, a disappointed God. And remembering God's thunderous response to the misdeeds of the wandering Israelites, I can understand how Grandma might crumble in the wake of death. Grandma must have seen God's law as a measure of her shortcomings. Moses knew God's law to be a measure of our worth. God cares enough to expect the best of us. God doesn't do mediocre. God raises the bar, but He doesn't just issue edicts from on high; He also provides a lane of grace in which to travel with us.

At Dad's memorial service, I read a psalm. I take great pleasure in knowing that I selected the very same Bible verses Dad had requested in notes we'd find later. After years and years of discord and division, we'd finally agreed on that which was so much more important, words that had meaning for us both.

I look to the hills! Where will I find help?

It will come from the Lord, who created heaven
and earth.

The Lord is your protector, and he won't go to sleep
or let you stumble.

The protector of Israel doesn't doze or ever get
drowsy.

The Lord is your protector, there at your right side
to shade you from the sun.
You won't be harmed by the sun during the day or
by the moon at night.
The Lord will protect you and keep you safe from
all dangers.
The Lord will protect you now and always wherever
you go.

Psalm 121 (CEV)

God's grace, that special lane in our travels in which we find Jesus waiting with outstretched arms. When the road narrowed, He was there for Grandma. He was there for Mom and Dad. He's also there for each one of us.

Rest Area

1. Have you been able to say good-bye to someone near death?

2. Do you see God's law as a measure of your short-comings or a measure of your worth?

3. Where has God's grace found you? How has God's grace changed you?

4. What's the difference between being your best and being the best? Any times when they're the same?

5. How have childhood struggles shaped your adult responses to life's challenges?

One Way

The Lord said, "I will go with you and give you peace."

Then Moses replied, "If you aren't going with us, please don't make us leave this place. But if you do go with us, everyone will know that you are pleased with your people and with me. That way, we will be different from the rest of the people on earth."

And the Lord told him, "I will do what you have asked, because I am your friend and I am pleased with you."

Then Moses said, "I pray that you will let me see you in all of your glory."

—Exodus 33:14-18 (CEV)

Chapter 9

"How do I get so mixed up?"

"Sir, I think you should've turned back there."

Shifting uncomfortably in the backseat of our New York City cab, I turned from the driver to my husband. "Kurt, why is he going straight? Why didn't he turn at the light?" For the second day in a row, I found myself challenged and confused by the Big Apple's crisscrossing streets and avenues. The first day I'd been so sure, so confident. Now I sat flustered and shaken as I looked out the cab's window at early morning traffic. *Where are we?*

I'd not been to New York since 1980 when I'd been a delegate to the Democratic National Convention. Even then, I'd been directionally challenged, turning east when I should've gone west, heading uptown when I'd wanted to go downtown. Now, feeling a little unnerved, I pressed on in a rather plaintive whisper, "Kurt, shouldn't he have turned back there?"

Kurt shook his head ever so slightly. No. Again, I was wrong. I'd wanted our cabbie to turn down a one-way street in the opposite direction of our destination, Rockefeller Center. Yesterday's driver had merely shrugged his shoulders and continued on his way. Today's driver glowered at me in his rearview mirror. He didn't need to be told how to navigate city streets by an anxious, misinformed traveler in his cab's backseat, especially a traveler who'd just flown in from the opposite coast, three time zones and eight states away.

"Kurt, how do I get so mixed up?"

Kurt tried to be supportive and instructive. "Remember, our hotel faces west. When you walk out the front door, you turn right to go north." Then he chuckled, "Too many tall buildings?"

Tall buildings were only a part of my problem. I was in a city of eight million people and I felt like I had eight million places to go with eight million ways to get there. I was overwhelmed and anxious. My navigational mistakes were reinforcing deep-rooted insecurities. Our long-awaited trip to the big city was going to end in frustration and disappointment, if I didn't let a few cab drivers guide me. There might be many different ways to our destination, but I needed just one way—the cabbie's.

I thought I'd been so informed. Our first day in New York, Kurt and I had taken a double-decker bus tour. I'd wanted to get my bearings and see the sites. Block after block I'd clung to my city map, trying to orient and reorient myself with each turn as we made our way through Manhattan and Harlem, the Theater District and Times Square, SoHo and Little Italy, neighborhoods and neighborhood attractions. When we got off the bus two and a half hours later, I'd looked at Kurt and asked, "Where are we?"

I don't like being unsure. I hate being lost. I fear not knowing where I am. My anxiety is often countered with an unreasonable and unwarranted seizure of the situation. I advise cab drivers even though I don't know where I am or where I'm going. Later I laugh at my silliness, but at times, it's not so funny. On one unrelated occasion I found myself in a situation that felt bigger than New York City traffic, one well beyond my ability to manage. While publishing my first book, I didn't just get a little disoriented on a one-way street; I lost my bigger sense of direction in my travels with God.

Holding a completed manuscript, I knew I needed help. My joy in writing had quickly given way to concern. I worried that I might make a wrong turn and head the project down a snarly, ego-driven path if I didn't get the right help and guidance. I risked misusing beautiful words and derailing an important message. For this very special project, I'd need to proceed one way—God's way.

I hadn't intended to write a book. I'd just wanted our adult sons, Kyle and Kevin, to know how I'd met their father. One summer's vacation had included both questions and snickers about possible scenarios, and I'd decided it was important to get the story down on paper, to preserve the memories. Kurt and I could easily have shared specifics over a pitcher of beer and a basket of drummettes, harkening back to those early days, but I'd wanted to put our family's history into a framework of God's love and faithfulness.

Returning home from our trip, I'd sat down at my computer and begun the tale. I wrote about the PLU party where I'd met the football player destined to become father to those two young men. Back in 1972, I thought Kurt was the cutest starter on the team, not exactly the best criteria for marital bliss, but my singular focus at the time. Like Kurt, I was a freshman. Unlike Kurt, I was a little ditzy with at least one of life's priorities out of alignment. Relying on the ringing endorsement of upper class friends, I'd waltzed into the room the night we met, stopped in front of him, and announced, "Hi, I'm Deanna. I'm supposed to like you." Responding to my exuberance, he'd replied, "Oh, really..."

While writing about that decisive time, I began to see how God had surrounded me with great care and much love, even at my ditziest, even as I struggled with life's priorities. When I finished the story about love, I began another, this one about self-discipline. Two more followed about peace and joy. I smiled as I watched the fruit of God's Holy Spirit emerge. Before writing, if you'd asked me about God's fruit, images of cartoon characters would've come to mind, a dancing peach, a singing banana, trite personifications of God's blessings. Now I began to see how the fruit of God's Spirit really had become the fruit of my own. By looking back and finding words for experiences I'd both treasured and trivialized, I'd been able to reframe life in God's grace.

The initial draft of my book done, moments of sheer joy and bouts of anxiousness bombarded me. *I've written a book.* At first cautious and unsure, it didn't take long before I was exclaiming to anyone within earshot, "I wrote a book!" Reading and rereading the manuscript, I felt grateful, yet humble, excited, yet uncertain. *I've written a book. I've really written a book.*

First, excitement. Then anxiety. *Now what?*

I'd expected the writing to be the hardest part of the whole undertaking, but the words had actually come quickly, easily. What stumped me was the publishing process. I'd edited the church newsletter and office communications, but nothing exceptionally noteworthy, nothing that was going to open publishing doors. And then I sensed another issue looming: creative production. In my mind I could see the finished book, the cover, the inside layout of each chapter, even the size. I knew what photos I wanted to include. Like the words He'd given me, God seemed to be leading me in the actual production of the book. I was both delighted and nervous. I wanted to honor and respect God's guidance, God's way, but the magnitude of the project troubled me. I seemed to be on audacious quest fraught with too many ways to mess up. "God, if I'm going to do this, if I'm going to publish a book, I'm going to need You with me. Every step of the way. *Every* step of the way."

And then one spring morning, God led me to Sue Collier. Her book, *The Complete Guide to Self-Publishing*, appeared to be the complete guide to self-publishing. Her website was a treasure trove for anyone wanting to self-publish. I didn't, but something about her obvious zeal for the publishing process resonated with me, and I knew I had to speak with her.

Calling the number on her website, I jokingly told Sue that what I really wanted were professionals to publish my book the way she'd told self-publishers to publish their own books. And then I replied in disbelief, "You can?" Sue said that she'd just put together a service and a team to help authors publish books. "You did?" Rereading the introduction to her *Complete Guide*, I chuckle at its opening question: "Are you the type of person who wants to be behind the wheel rather than just along for the ride?" Sue had been the right person at the right time. She'd understood and respected my hopes and dreams for the book.

Eight months later, I held my first copy of *Fruit of My Spirit: Reframing Life in God's Grace*. I was thrilled. I was over the moon. I carried the book with me everywhere. I read and reread it. I sat and held it close. I turned the pages and delighted in the pictures. God had truly blessed me with an enormous gift! An *enormous* gift!

The next day reality loomed. *Okay, now what?* Looking into a box of 100 books, I laughed in amusement. Obviously, my story was moving beyond two young men. The book was now available at Amazon, Barnes & Noble, and other websites. I also had my own website, an author's page on Facebook, and a couple signings scheduled. What possibilities!

What pitfalls! Remembering the wilderness en route to the Promised Land, I might have compared the size of my ego to Mount Sinai, but at only 7,500 feet, I'm not so sure. Being from the Pacific Northwest, a better measure is surely Mount Rainier at over 14,000 feet. I was so impressed with myself. My mind raced with possibilities. *Do I have time to make it to Oprah's couch before she ends her afternoon talk show?* I'd take my little book and go big for God. My husband had always encouraged his seventh-grade football teams to "Go big!" and now I wanted to go big, too. I built a spreadsheet and divided book proceeds between fifteen pet projects and dreamy dreams, getting the house painted and creating college funds for grandchildren I didn't yet have. Oh, yes, and at some point, I remembered to tithe.

Sitting on my own couch, I began promoting the book. Bloggers blogged about it; reviewers reviewed it. Soon my weeks were filled with stars—not the beautiful, twinkling, celestial bodies that brighten the night's sky, but the book rating system of Amazon, Barnes & Noble, and Goodreads. Each new day brought a new review, and each new review brought more stars. For six months I basked in the attention: "a writer I can relate to," "well written and honest," "so personal and so intimate with readers," "an engaging writer." I relished the praise, loved the wonderful things said about me, and delighted in thank-you notes and emails.

And then I was unexpectedly knocked from my egotistical pedestal. Eleven months after the release of *Fruit of My Spirit*, I'd arranged a book signing at the university bookstore where I'd gone to school. I got to be the featured guest for Parents' Weekend. Arriving early,

I followed the store's manager to a cozy meeting area next to the entry. She smiled and said the setup would be perfect for my signing with the room's small stage, café tables and chairs, and gas fireplace. Knowing people would be coming in from a cold football game, she pointed to the hot chocolate bar in the corner. "Have you ever seen homemade marshmallows? The school's kitchen staff actually makes them!"

No, I'd never seen homemade marshmallows, but I'd seen the small stack of books for the signing. Ten books. She'd ordered ten books for a two-hour event. After taking three away for pre-sales, I had seven. Seven. And a stack of paper for orders should we run out. Seven books.

An hour into the event, I looked at my small pile of books. In sixty minutes, I'd sold just one book, a pity sale to a mother who'd sat stirring a homemade marshmallow in her cocoa for the better part of forty-five minutes. Not sure where to throw her empty cup, she'd walked by my table and tried to make small talk.

"So what's your book about?"

"It's a memoir of short stories."

Feeling a chill in the air, she nodded, took a book, and hurried away.

A memoir of short stories? In the midst of a full-fledged pity party, I could only manage a terse reply. No warm, friendly greeting. No mom-to-mom bonding. Just a few words that an editor would eventually tell me were not even accurate. "You've got to quit saying that. Your book is not a collection of short stories," she admonished. "Short stories are a literary form with dramatic elements. That's not what you've written." Oh.

That afternoon in the bookstore, I could've said I'd written an inspirational memoir. I could've smiled and talked about memorable moments shared. I could've taken time to reframe life in God's grace. I could've grabbed a whipped, spongy square of white sugar from the hot chocolate bar and talked about the sweetness of God's love and faithfulness. I could've done so many things, but instead I pouted.

Feeling unsettled, flustered, and uneasy, I left my signing corner and wandered about the store. Standing between aisles of books, I finally admitted to being lost. I thought I'd known what I was doing. I didn't. I'd had no clue. Now feeling miserable, I returned to my little pile of six books and, taking my seat, began to realize where I'd gone wrong. I'd taken the promotion of my book and made it the promotion of me. I'd spent months celebrating what I'd done, not what God had done. I'd been so sure, so confident. I'd carefully worked my way through the writing and publishing of my book, but then I'd gotten distracted in the promotion of it. Without God and His direction, I'd had nothing to offer. I was just another author looking for shelf space and a chance at market share. I'd actually become "a resounding gong," "a clanging cymbal" (1 Corinthians 13:1).

The Israelites had also gotten off track when Moses was on Mount Sinai. Waiting for him to return from his meeting with God, they'd grown disillusioned and impatient. At the very moment Moses was getting the Ten Commandments, those rules for right living, they were deciding their own rules for living, taking matters into their own hands.

"What's happened to Moses? We need a god who can lead us!"

Unwilling to wait upon the God who'd brought them out of Egypt, the Israelites created a false god. Not willing to wait upon the God who'd helped me write a book, I created a false sense of self-worth. The Israelites sacrificed gold for an idol. I sacrificed time and energy for reviews. Our reasons seemed obvious: I told myself I was just trying to do a good job promoting the wonderful book God had given me. The Israelites said they were just trying to make sure they had a god to go before them. We were all just trying to find our way, but our hearts had turned in the wrong direction. We were all headed the wrong way, not the one way God had intended. Moses knew that without God he and the Israelites would not get far. That day in the bookstore, I learned the same. None of us would reach the Promised Land following false gods, whether golden calves or inflated egos.

After the golden calf incident, Moses reminded God that he'd been called for a special purpose, that the Israelites were part of a special relationship with Him.

"Without You, we're no different from anyone else."
—Moses

"God, You've told me to lead these people. You've told me that I'm special, that You know me by name. But, God, we've got to have you with us on this journey. Without You, we're no different from anyone else."

After my afternoon in the bookstore, I knew I had to regroup with God. I had to confess my pride and acknowledge my mistakes. In a Mosaic plea, I beseeched God, "I need help. You've given me the ability to write and connect with people, to tell of Your great glory. Please help me to get out of the way and let You lead." For this whole project to work, I had one way to go. With God. His way.

Six months after the book signing, my ego still reeling, my friend Claudia invited me to speak to the women at her church. God had given me another chance. Rather than sign books, we'd be talking about the fruit of God's Spirit. We met in a cozy meeting room next to the church entry. The setup was perfect with comfortable chairs arranged in a circle, a table of hors d'oeuvres, and a fireplace. It was an afternoon in which we got to tell of God's great love and faithfulness and share His most wonderful Spirit. Remembering our time together, I marvel at how the conversation captured hopes and dreams, frustrations and disappointments, how the women shared stumbles and victories in their walk with God. I watched women who'd worshipped together for five, ten, even twenty years connect on a new level, saying again and again, "Really? I didn't know that..." If asked, I'm not sure they'd even remember that I'd been there. Our time had been all about God and their own travels through life.

After the event, I went back to writing. I set aside the speaking brochures and focused on my second manuscript, connecting with Brenda Wilbee, author of the Seattle Sweetbriar Series and director of Literary (Service) Agency. I told her I wanted to become a better writer, and she took me at my word. Brenda got me refocused on God's message, telling me what I needed to hear, not what I wanted to hear. She pulled me through rewrites and challenged me to excel. She got chapters reorganized. She corrected verb tense and sharpened dialog. Taking my propensity to pontificate, she helped me hone my message, finding key words buried in a hasty conclusion. At times she hurt my feelings, bruised my ego. I'd whimper, wondering what was so wrong with a particular word, a favorite sentence. I'd carp to friends, "She's you're worst Comp101 professor!" She wasn't. She was an honest, caring critique for someone who'd asked to be part of something bigger and better.

Moses called upon God, knowing there was only one way for the people to go—God's way. Moses also knew the people wouldn't be able to go God's way without His help and guidance. God blessed the Israelites with commandments for right living and, in her own way, Brenda blessed me with commandments for right writing. With God's law in hand, Moses helped the Israelites understand who they were as God's people. Brenda helped me see a bigger purpose for me and my writing: to share stories of God's love and faithfulness, to share inspirational words of hope and promise, using my own vulnerabilities and missteps to begin the conversation. In their travels through the wilderness, God promised to be with Moses and the people every step of the way. In our own travels through life, God promises to be with us every step of the way. Moses helped the Israelites proceed one way—with God—His way. With Brenda's help, I was able to proceed one way, too—with God—His way. Remembering what Moses told God, that's how we're different from everyone else.

Rest Area

1. How can you "Go big!" for God without climbing an egotistical pedestal?

2. How has God gotten your attention when you've sounded like "a resounding gong" or "clanging cymbal?"

3. How do you know when you're headed God's way? When you're not?

4. Who has God put in your life to lead you? To re-direct you?

5. Who needs to hear your own story?

Scenic Viewpoint

"So now, revere the LORD. Serve him honestly and faithfully. Put aside the gods that your ancestors served beyond the Euphrates and in Egypt and serve the LORD. But if it seems wrong in your opinion to serve the LORD, then choose today whom you will serve. Choose the gods whom your ancestors served beyond the Euphrates or the gods of the Amorites in whose land you live. But my family and I will serve the LORD."

—Joshua 24:14-15 (CEV)

Chapter 10

"Oh, my! Big painting!"

"I said I'd be home by 11:00!" In response to a question about evening plans, I snapped back at my parents with a cheeky arrogance. Grabbing the keys to Dad's truck, I headed out, the door slamming behind me. I'd wanted to end the conversation with an exclamation point that would reverberate long after I'd left. I was off to a meeting at school, but after that, I had no plans. And even if I did, I didn't want to have to say. I was almost eighteen and going to college soon. I wanted to be independent, which for me meant unaccountable.

I climbed into the truck and started the engine, giving the gas pedal an extra rev, letting my frustration resound throughout the garage. Preparing to back out, I pulled the truck's gearshift forward and down a notch into reverse. With my foot still in "rev" mode, the truck lurched backward, and before I could brake, the right front bumper caught the garage door. The frame's narrow wood trim screeched and splintered. Throwing the gearshift back into park, I pushed open the door and swore in frustration. Stepping down, I turned to see my father standing on the other side of the driveway, arms folded across his chest, body tensed in anger.

"Oh, Dad, listen! I just—"

"No, Deanna, you listen."

He'd heard it all: the door slam, the engine rev, the wood crack, my swearing. He'd seen it all, too: my immaturity, my self-indulgence, my unrestrained attitude. From where he'd stood, he'd had a not-so-scenic viewpoint of a young woman flailing through adolescence. Now he'd seen enough. From his unique vantage point, he put life into perspective for me. "You're quick to grab keys for a truck you didn't buy, using gas you didn't pay for. You've been given much. You can walk, you know!"

During the Israelites' journey to the Promised Land, Joshua had seen and heard it all, too. Born in Egypt prior to their exodus, Joshua had followed Moses into the wilderness. He'd understood God's extraordinary call and experienced God's great faithfulness. He'd been allowed to approach Mount Sinai when Moses received the Ten Commandments. He'd even been selected to lead the Israelites after Moses' death.

Joshua had also known the Israelites' shortcomings. He'd heard their grumblings and seen their disobedience and short-sightedness. In many ways the Israelites had been flailing through their own adolescence as God's people. Like me, their behavior had, at times, been immature, their independent attitude unrestrained. Hot and thirsty, tired and hungry, they'd ended more than one conversation with an exclamation point! After settling into the Promised Land, Joshua was ready to use his unique vantage point to put their lives in perspective.

"God brought your fathers out of Egypt," Joshua reminded the Israelites. "God gave you land with cities you did not build, vineyards and olive groves you did not plant. Serve Him with faithfulness. Turn from other gods. Decide right now whom you will serve." He ended by declaring, "As for me and my house, we will serve the Lord."

Both Moses and Joshua had wanted the Israelites to keep life in perspective. How often we're asked to do the same. In the next breath, we're cautioned not to blow things out of proportion. One of my first lessons in perspective came in a driveway. Others would come later, the years providing a scenic viewpoint from which to gain a bigger, better perspective. Sightseeing also helped.

On our visit to New York City, Kurt and I saw as much as we could: Rockefeller Center and the Empire State Building, the USS

Intrepid and a tour boat, Times Square and Trinity Church. We enjoyed late night humor, modern art, and history. We attended a Broadway musical and an introduction to a new Broadway musical. We walked uptown and down. We took a carriage ride through Central Park. I bought no souvenirs, no postcards or mementos. What remained with me were memories and unexpected lessons in perspectives.

In New York, I'd expected to be regaled by the sights; I was in a "New York state of mind." The scenic viewpoints astounded me. I got to see New York from the deck of an aircraft carrier, the observatory of an iconic office tower, a boat in the harbor. What astounded me even more were the scenic viewpoints I'd enjoy from inside the city's theaters and museums. There I got lessons in perspective that would remain with me long after flying home, lessons that would come from two inspirational entertainers and three nineteenth-century painters.

Jimmy Fallon's one of my favorite comedians. I like his humor. His jokes capture the hilarity of our crazy times; his one-liners leave me laughing out loud. I especially appreciate his ability to entertain without being crass, to charm without throwing a guest under the bus. He's a classy entertainer who ends Friday night shows with on-air thank-you notes. What's not to like?

Before our trip, I'd tried to reserve seats for a Jimmy Fallon taping. Tickets were not available, but prior to the show, he'd be running through his monologue before a live audience. Those tickets were available. Monday afternoon Kurt and I found ourselves sitting in the second row of Studio 6A listening to Fallon rehearse. Pen and paper in hand, he checked off jokes about the recent government shutdown, the relighting of the Olympic torch, online dating. For seven minutes we laughed at headlines that had screamed for our attention. Fallon made us smile, and in a humorous way, he'd put the day's events into perspective. Laughing at his own jokes, he'd reminded us that life didn't need to be taken so seriously, despite what CNN and Fox News might report, despite "What's Trending" on social media. Lesson one.

Lesson two came a couple nights later at a Sting benefit concert. Sitting beside Kurt in The Public Theater, I was ecstatic! Months earlier I'd spent an entire afternoon scoring tickets. I'd talked *ad nauseam* about my good fortune to family, friends, and casual acquaintances, even a store cashier. I was going to be *a mere twenty feet* from my favorite rock star! I hummed "Roxanne" and "Every Breath You Take."

But neither song was sung. Opening the show, Sting told the audience he'd be performing original material for the first time in ten years. *What? No "Brand New Day?"* No *"Message in a Bottle?"* Sting talked about his struggles with writer's block, about his need to grow as an artist and a person, to take an inward perspective and move creatively forward. He then spent the evening introducing his new Broadway play, *The Last Ship.* Sitting taller in his seat, he recounted the story of a proud, hardworking town building its last big ship. He spoke passionately, sang movingly. Interwoven throughout the dialog and lyrics were people and places from Sting's own childhood in a shipbuilding community. Fallon had shown me that life doesn't always have to be taken so seriously, and now Sting had shown me how important it is to remember the stories of others as well as our own.

My third lesson in perspective started with a rainstorm, a torrential downpour that sent Kurt and I running for cover inside the Museum of Modern Art. With only forty-five minutes until closing, I pointed Kurt to the elevator. "Van Gogh!" We had six floors of exhibits, but I had one priority, an 1889 oil painting.

We weren't the only visitors escaping the elements, nor were we the only ones wanting to enjoy favorite modern masters. The museum was packed with art aficionados, school-aged sightseers, and tourists. Weaving through the crowds, I checked the time on my watch. Twenty minutes. I picked up my pace, hurrying from gallery to gallery, giving Pop Art masterpieces a cursory glance, nodding briefly at a Jackson Pollock drip painting. When a voice came over the speaker warning us that the museum would be closing soon, my body tensed. *Where is it?*

After wandering off in a different direction, I looked up to see Kurt walking toward me. "Did you see it?" he asked.

"Van Gogh? No! Have you?"

Kurt pointed to a narrow wall directly behind me in the center of the room. Hanging alone, surrounded by a quiet group of captivated onlookers, was Vincent van Gogh's *The Starry Night*. Unexpected tears slipping down my cheeks, I stared in wonder at a small painting of bold, beautiful colors, a landscape of nighttime quiet and heavenly intensity, artwork that invoked both awe and sadness. I stepped closer. The painting was not at all what I'd expected. I'd expected something large—huge, in fact—a painting that would command attention, not a vibrant, but smaller work of art. I'd certainly not expected this smaller glimpse into artistic genius and creativity.

Days later Kurt and I visited the Metropolitan Museum of Art. Again we wandered from gallery to gallery, this time moving from Egyptian relics to contemporary art, from photographs to sculptures. After an hour, I said to Kurt, "I want to see *Washington Crossing the Delaware*."

Grabbing our map, we set off for Gallery 760. We looked and looked and walked and walked. Finally seeing a museum attendant, I asked for directions. With a funny look on his face, he turned his head over his left shoulder and let his eyes point to the wall behind him.

"Oh, my!" I laughed. "Big painting!"

There, right in front of me, hung the huge canvas of George Washington's 1776 attack on the Hessians at Trenton. Like van Gogh's *The Starry Night*, Emanuel Leutze's 1851 painting was not what I'd expected. This one was enormous! The canvas took up the entire wall! Walking from end to end, I marveled at detailed brushstrokes that took me back to high school history where I'd first learned about a battle that had defined our country.

What a lesson in perspective! One painting was diminutive compared to my expectations, one much larger. With van Gogh, I'd marveled at the smallness of a huge masterpiece. With Leutze, I'd stood in awe of a painting's detailed enormity. Neither was as I imagined. Their unexpected beauty, color, and size inspired awe and wonder, pulling me closer and pushing me back in my study of each, in my appreciation of both. In life I'd need to do the same.

Hitting the garage door has loomed large in my mind for four decades. In reality, the incident was a smaller mishap from my all-about-me-all-the-time teenage years. I'd driven carelessly through adolescence, a dented right fender and frustrated father reminders of the journey. In life's gallery of events, my afternoon of cheeky arrogance was a smaller picture on a narrow wall. And certainly no masterpiece!

> "Life is not measured by the number of breaths we take,
> but by the moments that take our breath away."
> —Maya Angelou

Lessons in perspective. First, Jimmy Fallon had reminded me to laugh, joking that life doesn't need to be taken so seriously. Sting had iterated in words and songs the importance of our collective stories, our shared history. And then there were Vincent van Gogh and Emanuel Leutze whose artwork had inspired both awe and wonder. Maya Angelou once said, "Life is not measured by the number of breaths we take, but by the moments that take our breath away." In his own way, each had taken my breath away.

My fourth lesson in perspective would be tied to a lesson in faith. Walking into a longer, narrower gallery at MoMA, I looked across the room to see Claude Monet's long, narrow painting "Water Lilies." Standing beside the artwork, I was surprised to find that I couldn't see the actual picture, only dashes of color and intricate brushstrokes. Not until I stepped to the other side of the room could I see the famous lily pond, the reflection of clouds. Up close I saw only dabs of black paint, splotches of blue and purple, pink and yellow. From a distance, I could see depth and shadows. Standing back, I could see a peaceful Japanese-style pond covered with beautiful lilies, an overcast sky visible in the shimmering water.

Monet's masterpiece was huge—three panels, each six feet by more than thirteen feet, forty-one feet total. I shook my head wondering how he'd painted something so large. At arm's length, the landscape was indistinguishable. Standing at the canvas, paint-brush in hand, Monet would have seen nothing but swirls of paint, yet he'd been able to blend three-dimensional strokes of carefully chosen colors in exquisite, yet simple, detail, creating a strikingly beautiful masterpiece.

Monet had known about perspective. His artistic eye had beheld not just flowers in a pond but light and color, depth and distance, shadow and movement of floating botanical beauties in waters that looked both mysterious and inviting. He'd also known about faith. Up close, he couldn't have seen the images, yet with a faith in his professional aptitude, he'd been able to mix wisdom and experience on a well-used palette of oil paints, his eyes seeing in confidence what his hands would create with assurance.

What perspective! What faith! Recalling Joshua's admonish-ment to the Israelites, what a lesson! Confidence in what we hope for and assurance about what we do not see. At times I've been so close to life's artwork I haven't been able to make out the picture. During adolescence and throughout life, I've needed to step back in order to see the bigger picture. I've needed lessons in perspective. Life includes humor, the stories and experiences of others, awe, wonder, and faith. At times my vision's been limited, my viewpoint restricted to a particular time and place. But in life, I've also been given the chance to swirl together wisdom and experience, knowing God will guide the brush. In God I can have that confidence and assurance.

My friend Nancy shared a poignant lesson in perspective and faith after the tragic loss of her 23-year-old grandson. When he died, the picture seemed bleak, and I asked God to be with her and her family. I prayed they might have strength and guidance, love and support in their time of mourning. Over coffee several weeks later, I asked Nancy how she was doing. Her eyes still reflecting pain and grief, she replied, "You know, God has been with us in so many ways." Nancy told us how she'd actually been in town visiting her daughter and family when they learned of his death. Together they'd been able to support each other and work through funeral arrangements, planning his memorial service, crying in anguish, and smiling in remembrance of a dearly loved young man.

Nancy had stood just feet from death, figurative dark spots of color before her, metaphorical brush strokes trailing black across life's canvas. But there she was taking a symbolic step to other side of the room. Seeing the bigger picture in the midst of her sorrow and loss, she was watching God's faithfulness emerge from the darkest, most tragic landscape.

Days later, my heart still hurting for Nancy, Kurt and I had lunch with my son Kevin and his new wife, Manoela. Feeling conflicted about my joy and Nancy's grief, I asked Kurt about blessings. Our sons had loving, joyous marriages, their wives enriching our lives in ways we never could've imagined. "Kurt, what does God want us to do with the good times?"

Driving home that day, we reminded each other to appreciate our blessings, to thank God for all that we'd been given. Now I wonder if the answer also lies in the artwork of an Impressionist master and a friend's walk through grief. Perhaps our good times are when we "move across the room" in life and marvel at the wonderful masterpiece before us. Those beautiful moments become lessons in perspective. They give us confidence and assurance, because the time will come when life happens, when we'll be just feet from dark spots of color, when we'll need to find our way back across the room in order to see the lilies.

My father was a talented artist. His oil paintings grace the homes of family and friends. I didn't inherit his talent, but standing in the driveway as a seventeen-year-old, I benefited from his perspective. Lessons have continued throughout my life. Yes, even while sightseeing. God's been with me, at times holding the paintbrush, selecting the colors, helping me to get the shading just right, at other times walking with me across the room where I've been able to see a most divine masterpiece. For each of us, the viewpoints and perspectives are unique, but together with God, we walk in faith, that confidence in what we hope for and assurance about what we do not see.

Rest Area

1. Where is your favorite scenic viewpoint?
2. Where have you gotten the best lessons in perspective?
3. Has an incident from your past loomed large for too long?
4. How has God put life in perspective for you?
5. Where have you needed to "move across the room" in order to see life's masterpiece?

Construction Zone

Moses, the LORD's servant, was dead. So the LORD spoke to Joshua son of Nun, who had been the assistant of Moses. The LORD said:

"Long ago I promised the ancestors of Israel that I would give this land to their descendants. So be strong and brave! Be careful to do everything my servant Moses taught you. Never stop reading The Book of the Law he gave you. Day and night you must think about what it says."

"I've commanded you to be strong and brave. Don't ever be afraid or discouraged! I am the LORD your God, and I will be there to help you wherever you go."

—Joshua 1:1, 5-7, 9 (CEV)

Chapter 11

"How are we doing on time?"

Uh oh! Looking into my rearview mirror, I watched the motorcycle, lights flashing, slip in behind me. Seconds earlier I'd caught sight of the radar gun but thought nothing of it. I was only going fifty-five, not even my usual "four over." I was actually keeping pace with six other cars on my way to the airport and, together with my in-laws, I wouldn't have thought to speed.

I pulled over to the shoulder, stopped, and grabbed my license and the car's registration. My father-in-law looked out the back window. "Would you like me to speak with him? Perhaps if he knew we had a flight to catch..."

My father-in-law was worried. This seemingly minor stop posed a not-so-minor threat to our travel plans. Sadly, I knew there was nothing minor about my traffic infractions. I tried to sound reassuring, "I'm not exactly sure what this is all about. Let's see what he has to say. Don't worry. We've still got plenty of time to get to the airport."

I took a deep breath and rolled down my window. "Good morning, sir."

From behind dark sunglasses, the officer couched down and began, "Were you aware that you were going 55 in a 40?"

A 40 MPH zone?

"You're actually in a construction zone."

A construction zone? I looked around. Orange barrels lined the highway, had lined the highway for two miles. I flinched. I should've known better. Orange barrels were an everyday occurrence in the greater Seattle area. Our tax dollars were at work repaving roads, straightening curves, redirecting traffic. In addition to barrels, there'd been orange signs asking us to GIVE 'EM A BRAKE and PREPARE TO STOP. But again I'd missed the signs.

Speed and inattention have clearly become stubborn themes in my life. Now add my inability to embrace change. I've never been excited to see orange barrels and cones. I don't like orange signs slowing me down. But those orange traffic control signs and devices mark areas of change, places where I really do need to slow down. Life changes, too. And if we're not cautious, if we're not heeding those orange alerts both on the highway and in life, we risk slamming into the changes ahead of us. Too often I've had my foot on the accelerator, speeding to my destination, not watching for signs, not looking for changes. If I'd just slow down, I'd see that those orange signs are frequently alerting me to something new and better, something I can get excited about! On our way to the airport, the county was widening the road, adding new lanes in each direction. Orange barrels would also mark new and exciting changes to our family. Two years ago, the four of us became six when Kyle married Katie and Kevin married Manoela. On our way to both ceremonies, Kurt and I actually drove through road construction projects. Not only would the two of us need to slow down as we maneuvered around orange barrels, but one of us would also need to slow down at the events themselves.

Kyle's wedding fell on a warm fall afternoon. Heading to the venue, I'd had no time to "Ooh!" and "Aah!" over the red, yellow and orange foliage lining our route. My focus had been the road and our destination. Highway 2 was under construction with complex closures and detours. I'd asked Kurt to leave well ahead of schedule to accommodate possible delays. Really, I just wanted to get there as quickly as possible. I couldn't wait for pictures! I couldn't wait for the wedding! I was giddy with anticipation! I was not about to be late!

"Kurt, how are we doing on time? I'm just so excited for Kyle and Katie! What a beautiful day! I just love Katie and just love that she loves our son. And Kevin will be there with Manoela! Oh, Kurt, isn't she just a delight? To know that our sons are loved and adored, isn't that just the best? Isn't it exciting to think about having these two wonderful ladies as part of our family? Okay, okay, I know Kevin's just starting to date Manoela, but this feels different. This feels serious. Do you see it, too? Kurt, how are we doing on time...?"

On and on I talked. I talked about our changing family. I talked about Kyle and the beautiful, young woman he was about to marry. Kyle had known Katie since high school. They'd reconnected after years apart, becoming best friends. We were thrilled that Katie was about to become an official part of our family. *"Kurt, how are we doing on time...?"* My excitement continued to pick up speed, but before the evening's end, I'd need to take my foot off the gas.

Exactly thirty minutes before the start of the service, I found myself pacing—from the entry to windows overlooking the entry, from the reception area to the great room, from the hallway inside to the parking circle outside. I was looking for the harpist who'd gotten delayed, fretting about a situation over which I had no control, a situation that would actually resolve itself minutes later when the harpist walked into the room and groaned, "Traffic!"

After the service, I was pacing again, this time checking that the ballroom's "flip" to the dinner set-up was on schedule. Checking my wristwatch for the umpteenth time, I wondered what could be taking so long. I caught myself working through a mental to-do list for an event that was neither mine to manage, nor one that even needed any particular time parameters. We had the entire evening to celebrate.

Without having to pull me over and issue a citation, family and friends helped me slow down. First, Kurt came alongside, stopping me before I collided with the wait staff. He winked and said, "Deanna, it's just perfect. Everything's just perfect." Knowing smiles and encouraging words also came from two church friends who'd graciously consented to facilitate the evening's flow, arriving early and staying late. "Deanna, it's fabulous! We've got this!" And then, "There's nothing to worry about, girlfriend!" With their help, I'd found the brakes.

Ten months later Kevin married Manoela as the sun set over the waters of Alki Beach. Again we found ourselves navigating a construction zone. The Spokane Street Viaduct of the West Seattle Bridge was undergoing major revisions with the addition of new on- and off-ramps and travel lanes. Orange barrels lined the road. In the confusion, our limo driver missed the turn and not surprisingly, I started to fret. We were going to be late. Focused on the time, I didn't see that the extra minutes were giving Manoela and her girlfriends time to laugh and be together. Kevin and the guys were hanging out on the pier. When we finally gathered for the wedding, the guys were relaxed, the girls happy. We came together in the coolness of a late summer evening, the splash of an incoming tide serenading Kevin and Manoela, an old dock supporting new love.

After the ceremony, we celebrated at the restaurant next door. So far I'd been pretty cool, calm, and collected, but waiting for our meal, I was back on the accelerator. Our dinner for seventeen had become a three-hour soiree. Anxious about the incredibly long time between our salads and the main course, my mind raced: *What's going on? Why the delay? Where's our server? Who's in charge here?*

Is that my steak sitting all by itself on a serving tray getting cold?

I was speeding through another beautiful construction zone when it hit me. Looking around the table, candlelight illuminating Kevin and Manoela's happiness, I heard it—that wee small voice that God uses to prick our consciousness. *Deanna, slow down—now! You're in no rush. Really! No rush! You're celebrating your son's marriage. You've got time. You've got the entire evening.* Finally I pulled up on the gas pedal and found the brakes. I settled back into my seat, looked around the table, and smiled. Yes, my son was married!

Leaving the restaurant hours later, we looked around at the vacated room. Our waitress was setting up for the next day's lunch; the hostess was grabbing a vacuum. Walking out, Kevin asked, "Mom, did dinner take a really long time?"

"Yes, Kevin, it did. But it was okay. It gave us more time to be together. Tonight was all about you and Manoela. We were in no rush."

No rush. Our family was changing, and we'd all need to slow down, especially me. Earlier a police officer had needed me to slow down and pay attention driving through a construction zone. Proceeding through two very special construction zones in our family's travels together, I'd also need to slow down and pay attention, to focus on the moment. I'd need to be present. Two weddings were changing our family, changes I'd miss if I focused on "doing," rather than "being."

The Israelites had to focus on "being," too. Before they entered the Promised Land, God spoke with their new leader Joshua on the side of the road, not to cite him, but to give him encouragement and exhortation. "Joshua, I will always be with you. Be strong and brave. Don't ever be afraid or discouraged. I am the LORD your God, and I will be there to help you wherever you go."

God had needed Joshua and the people to slow down. Lanes of travel and on- and off-ramps being added to lives that had circled through the desert on a hot and dusty path for forty years. The Israelites must have thought their journey was almost over. Finally! After a long and arduous trek through the wilderness, they were almost there! But nearing the Promised Land, God knew the people would need to stay alert and focused. In this particular construction zone, there'd be no orange barrels lining the road, just a divine Flagger alerting them to the important changes ahead. They'd need to unpack, find housing, get the kids settled, and the animals tended. They'd need to adjust from a nomadic lifestyle to a settled one. How would they live? Worship? "Proceed with caution," God exhorted.

Lives under construction. New directions, new journeys, new possibilities. Changes. God promised Joshua He would be with the Israelites while they navigated the new terrain: "Don't be afraid or discouraged! I will be there to help you." Their journey would continue, not just to the Promised Land, but through the Promised Land—and God would be with them.

God reminds us, "I will be with you wherever you go."

Change is difficult. Change is messy. Personally, I hate the inconvenience, the delays and detours. Going home after taking my in-laws to the airport, I carefully maneuvered through orange barrels, and then to my dismay, I missed another new off-ramp! Even with the help of orange signs, I'd gone off-course—again. Life's like that. We can make mistakes even while paying attention. Until the road's complete, we're never quite sure where we're going, but God reminds us, "I will be with you wherever you go." He's promised.

Right after that missed off-ramp, I passed another orange sign, END WORK ZONE. Unlike the construction zone, God's work never ends. Each day brings change—some planned and others not, some that surprise us and others that leave us feeling a little unsettled and uncomfortable. Some changes, like weddings, are easier to embrace. Others are harder. Some changes are downright challenging. Throughout we'll need to slow down and remain alert. At times we might miss an exit, speed through an event, but God promises to be with us. God gives us confidence and encouragement as we travel forward with Him. And when we're going too fast, when we miss the signs, God gets us refocused.

In a favorite children's book, Pooh asks Piglet, "What day is it?"

"It's today," squeaks Piglet.

"My favorite day," says Pooh.

When my sons were small, a rainy day was often their favorite. At the end of our driveway was a section of asphalt outlined in orange paint, a dip identified by the city for repair, but in the meantime, a dip that created the most marvelous puddle for two little boys when it rained. In the middle of a cloud burst, Kyle and Kevin would pull on their boots, strap on bicycle helmets, and peddle with abandon through the waters of their imagination. Covered in rain, dripping in mud, Kevin would stop, turn his bike, and cry out to his big brother, "Again!"

Two little boys just being two little boys. Just being. You and I may not be able to peddle with abandon through life's confusing and complicated construction zones, but we can learn to smile at the orange signs and imagine the possibilities to come. We can "be" because God is with us.

Because God is with us wherever we are and wherever we're going.

Rest Area

1. Do you find constructions zones a challenging nuisance? Exciting signs of change? Both?
2. Where have you passed by orange barrels and signs in your travels with God?
3. Any times in life when you've traveled too quickly?
4. How is your life under construction at this very moment?
5. How can you make sure to just "be" as a person of God?

Divided Highway

"For I know the plans I have for you," declares the LORD, "plans to prosper you and not to harm you, plans to give you hope and a future."

—Jeremiah 29:11 (NIV)

Epilogue

"God's speed."

Now the road divides for you and me. Here we part, you traveling with God in one direction and me in another. The Talmud says God leads where we choose to go. I would add that God leads where we've chosen to go and also where we haven't. There are times when He pulls us along, other times when He's gently nudging, times when we cry and whine, times when we celebrate and rejoice, moments when we miss the significance, moments when we actually stop and say, "Wow!"

> God leads where we've chosen to go
> and also where we haven't.

Heading down the road, you'll see very quickly that life never unfolds one sign at a time. In Monroe, the highway's edged with signs of all shapes and sizes, sandwich boards leaning in every direction, neon lights flashing, traffic alerts lost in the mix. Some signs are widely spaced, others sit on top of each other. Writing, I got to focus on one sign at a time, but like a cluttered highway, life has a plethora of signs, some widely spaced, some sitting on top of each other. Some grab our attention; others slip by unnoticed. Our challenge is to stay focused and proceed with caution, to see the signs and God's direction in our travels. He's promised to be with us—wherever we are, wherever we're going.

Remember, too, that your own story's as important as mine. At a book signing, a church friend Irene approached me, and with a shy smile, her eyes sparkling, she said, "I have a story to tell." She told about her family who emigrated from Norway, first to Canada and then to the United States. Her father died just after their arrival. With five children in tow, the youngest only a year old, her mother embraced a new life in the land of promised opportunity. Irene said her own father had been their Moses, leading them from the old country to a new one. She added that her mother had been their Joshua. Then she looked away and said, "I could never write a book." Perhaps not, but then not all stories will be written. Some will be shared at dinner with children and great-grandchildren; others will tumble out over coffee.

Our stories don't have to be found somewhere between Genesis and Revelation to matter. They don't have to appear on Amazon's best-seller list to count. Our stories are more important than that, because they're chapters in God's great story. Richard Rohr, a Franciscan friar, said, "The genius of the biblical story is that, instead of simply giving us 'seven habits for highly effective people,' it gives us permission and even direction to take conscious ownership of our own story at every level, every part of life and experience. God will use all of this material, even the negative parts, to bring life and love."

In the New Testament, Luke tells of two men walking to the town of Emmaus shortly after Jesus' resurrection. A third person joins them, but not until later do the men realize they've been traveling with Jesus. "Then their eyes were opened and they recognized him..." (Luke 24:31). It's easy to miss God in the moment. While writing, I expected to share a few driving antics and lessons learned. Instead I got to share travels in life and God's divine direction. He's been with me throughout, directing and redirecting. He's been with you, too.

Jeremiah was a man called to prophetic ministry six centuries after Moses and Joshua. Speaking to the Israelites, he gave voice to

God's word: *"For I know the plans I have for you, plans to prosper you and not to harm you, plans to give you hope and a future."* God's plans give us hope. His plans give meaning and purpose to our life. You and I have that promised future, knowing God is with us, directing and redirecting.

God's speed, my friend!

CPSIA information can be obtained
at www.ICGtesting.com
Printed in the USA
FSOW03n2048100615
7802FS